"A goldmine of valuable information! A no-nonsense approach to the fundamentals of sound financial planning. This step-by-step guide will help people take charge of their lives and build a solid financial future."

Doreen Roadman
Financial adviser, JJSA Advisors, Ltd., Virginia Beach, Virginia

"Making money in today's world is a piece of cake—if you have the right tools and a solid foundation. This book is a great resource to get you started on a new path of opportunity."

Tom Antion
Author, *The Ultimate Guide to Electronic Marketing for Small Business*

"Carolyn has done a great job addressing the large, intimidating subjects, such as budgeting and retirement planning, and made them easy to understand and act on. This book answers the same questions my clients ask almost daily in my practice as a certified financial planner. This book should be read by anyone who wants a better understanding of finance without the task of becoming an expert."

Carl R. Pierson, Jr.
Certified financial planner, Smith Barney, Inc.

"Carolyn has taken the many complexities of finance and stripped away their intimidating nature by providing clear, concise, and easily understood explanations and suggestions. With this book, anyone can gain the confidence they need to build their financial future."

Kim Pate
Vice president, Mortgage Lending with Towne Bank Mortgage

"Firmly grounded in faith, this excellent financial guide shows how to build your house on stone. Carolyn has written a comprehensive yet easy-to-read book. I wish I had this years ago."

Elizabeth Arnold

Author, *Creating the Goodwill* and Founder of Sowing Seeds

"If you've got financial questions, Carolyn has answers. This book is comprehensive, easy to follow, and practical. No matter what your level of financial knowledge, this is a resource every woman needs."

Dr. Linda Mintle

Therapist, speaker, and author of *Making Peace with Your Thighs*

"Carolyn Castleberry's *Women, Get Answers About Your Money* is comprehensive! A power-packed, practical guidebook all women can glean help and hope from!"

Pam Farrel

Bestselling author of more than twenty-six books including
10 Best Decisions a Woman Can Make and
Men are like Waffles, Women are like Spaghetti

"A very practical guide that will help women get smart fast when it comes to their finances."

Peggy Klaus

Author of *Brag! The Art of Tooting Your Own Horn Without Blowing It*

WOMEN, GET ANSWERS ABOUT YOUR MONEY

CAROLYN CASTLEBERRY

Multnomah Publishers

WOMEN, GET ANSWERS ABOUT YOUR MONEY
published by Multnomah Publishers
A division of Random House, Inc.
published in association with Ambassador Literary Agency, Nashville, TN

Unless otherwise indicated, Scripture quotations are from:
New American Standard Bible® © 1960, 1977, 1995
by the Lockman Foundation. Used by permission.
Other Scripture quotations are from:
The Holy Bible, New International Version (NIV)© 1973, 1984 by International Bible Society,
used by permission of Zondervan Publishing House
The Message © 1993, 1994, 1995, 1996, 2000, 2001, 2002
Used by permission of NavPress Publishing Group
Contemporary English Version (CEV) © 1995 by American Bible Society
The New Life Version (NLV) © Christian Literature International, 1969
Holy Bible, New Living Translation (NLT)
© 1996. Used by permission of Tyndale House Publishers, Inc. All rights reserved.

Multnomah is a trademark of Multnomah Publishers and is registered in the U.S. Patent and Trademark Office. The colophon is a trademark of Multnomah Publishers.

Printed in the United States of America

For information:
MULTNOMAH PUBLISHERS
12265 Oracle Boulevard, Suite 200 • Colorado Springs, CO 80921

Library of Congress Cataloging-in-Publication Data
Castleberry, Carolyn.
  Women, get answers about your money / Carolyn Castleberry.
      p. cm.
  Includes bibliographical references (p.   ) and index.
  ISBN 1-59052-799-2
  1. Women—Finance, Personal. 2. Finance, Personal. I. Title.
HG179.C3544 2006
332.0240082—dc22

                                            2006027955

06 07 08 09 10 11—10 9 8 7 6 5 4 3 2 1 0

To all the women who asked, "What's next?"
after *Women, Take Charge of Your Money*

Contents

I Wish I Had Asked the Dumb Questions

It was the summer of 1995, just months after our first daughter was born. I sat in a well-known financial expert's office clenching and unclenching my fists, reflecting on the realization that my husband and I desperately needed financial guidance. I had come alone.

My husband, John, is one of those men who would rather drive in circles for hours than stop and ask a stranger for directions. He had also resisted asking anyone for a financial road map. I, on the other hand, have no problem asking for directions. When God created me, He forgot to include an innate sense of direction and I sometimes use a global positioning system just to find my way from one child's soccer game to another child's birthday party. I wanted help. So off I went to meet with the financial adviser.

At the time, I worked as a reporter for an NBC affiliated station; asking questions was just part of my job. Sometimes even dumb, humiliating questions. If asking dumb questions didn't bother me on TV, why did I feel paralyzed and intimidated sitting in this man's office? I knew enough to ask for help, but I was afraid to ask for an education, so I could actively participate in the management of our money. I have three college degrees, including one in business, but every question I thought of sounded, well,... idiotic.

So I deferred to the "expert."

"Don't worry, Carolyn. Just let me handle your savings, and I'll make it work for you." His face said more: *All of this investing stuff is really over your head anyway.* Trusting person that I was, I wrote a check and handed him our money.

Over the subsequent months we watched thousands of dollars disappear in a series of trades, commissions, and margin calls, making him richer and us poorer. So much for the financial expert.

Was I wrong to ask for directions? No. The problem was that I was asking the wrong person. Or rather, I failed to ask the right Person. An eye-opening theory on Wall Street maintains that a monkey tossing darts at a target will outperform most financial advisers. But there's an Adviser who never fails. The God of all resources—Jesus Christ. If you think it's inappropriate to consult God about your financial life, think again. The Lord says we don't have what we want and need simply because we don't ask. (See James 4:2.)

How do you feel about asking God for wisdom concerning something as controversial as money? The Bible makes it clear that we're not to seek money just for money's sake. "Lust for money brings trouble and nothing but trouble. Going down that path, some lose their footing in the faith completely and live to regret it bitterly ever after" (1 Timothy 6:10, *The Message*). Instead, our focus should be on what money can do. Continuing in that same chapter: "Tell those rich in this world's wealth to quit being so full of themselves and so obsessed with money, which is here today and gone tomorrow. Tell them to go after God, who piles on all the riches we could ever manage—to do good, to be rich in helping others, to be extravagantly generous. If they do that, they'll build a treasury that will last, gaining life that is truly life" (1 Timothy 6:17–19, *The Message*)

Be extravagantly generous. I like that. And truly, it was learning to let go of fear and give to others that made the biggest difference in my financial life. That also means learning to trust. It's the Lord who allows us to prosper. If God accounts for every hair on your head, certainly He's willing to help you with the numbers associated with your financial future. The Bible makes it clear that we're not to put anything, including money, above Him on our priority list. But the Word of God also helps us understand that God hasn't left us alone to manage our finances. He has given us role models, stories, and principles to help us become good stewards of that most frightening, conflict-ridden, stress-inducing area of life—money.

As a reporter, I might have guessed that it would all come back to asking questions. Asking God for wisdom and power to live abundantly. Asking specific questions about how to achieve financial goals. Sometimes it's the seemingly dumb questions that elicit the most valuable answers, saving us the most money.

So I'm going to help you ask a lot of questions. And none of them are dumb. The only dumb thing is losing money because of prideful silence. Like when I walked out of that financial adviser's office.

Fortunately, I've grown wiser and more willing to admit I don't have all of the answers. What answers I do have, I've found because I'm not afraid to keep asking. I've learned to follow the model God has given us in the Proverbs 31 woman.

CREATE, CONSIDER, AND INVEST

After writing my first book, *Women, Take Charge of Your Money,* I met a Sunday school teacher who looked at me skeptically. "You've got to be kidding!" he said, "There's actually a woman in the Bible who was taking charge of her money?"

Yes, there is. Take a look at Proverbs chapter 31, verses 10–31. Here, in my own words, are a few bullets from the example of this investor and entrepreneur.

- She put God at the top of her priority list (verse 30).
- She made family her next priority (verses 21, 28).
- She maintained a positive outlook (verse 25).
- She put her creative talents to work (verses 13, 24).
- She was a careful investor (verse 16).
- She was a hard worker (verse 19).
- She was generous (verse 20).
- She was tough (verses, 15, 17–18, 25).
- She reaped positive rewards (verses 11, 31).

Not bad for a lady who lived in an age that was less kind to females than ours—one that didn't afford them all the opportunities we have now. She juggled relationships and career, and she took it one step further: She became an investor. An investor in God, in her family, and in business. She also invested in real estate—her field of dreams that would provide financially for her family long into the future.

In the Proverbs 31 woman we also have an easy model for investing that anyone can apply: Create, Consider, and Invest. She used her creative talents to build a business. She considered her field of investment. And only then did she invest.

In my first book I provided an in-depth look at this remarkable biblical model, focusing especially on *whom* to look to and *why* we should care. But soon after writing it, I began to receive lots of questions about *how* to follow this woman's example. The nuts and bolts. So I've developed this resource guide, again directing the information toward women, because studies show many of us need help in this area. Some women are brilliant money managers. This book is for the rest of us.

Part I will help you get your financial act together by first getting your own house in order, then successfully managing the stumbling blocks most of us encounter, and finally building a team you can trust.

Part II will help you consider your field of investment—whether it's market investing, your own business, intellectual property, or my favorite field of investing: real estate.

Part III will take a hard look at the end result of investment, dealing with the questions surrounding your retirement.

If you don't feel like a financial success, don't worry. This book will serve as a comprehensive resource, addressing the simple questions most people are afraid to broach. This is not meant to replace your bedtime novel or summertime beach read. It's a reference guide to help you, like the Proverbs 31 woman, consider your field of investment. And that begins with information.

So, my friend, let's go out and inspect your field…one question at a time.

PART I

Before You Invest

CHAPTER ONE

The Least You Need to Know About Your Money

But remember the LORD your God, for it is he who gives you the
ability to produce wealth, and so confirms his covenant,
which he swore to your forefathers, as it is today.
DEUTERONOMY 8:18, NIV

Do you realize that the person who makes the biggest difference in your financial future is *you*? Others can provide all kinds of great advice and opportunities to invest or run a business, but if you don't take action, nothing happens. In this book I can teach you how to manage your money, stick to a budget, find better investments and make wiser choices. But if all you do is read, nothing will change for you.

You can pray, and God is very willing to work powerfully in your financial life. But even He requires you to take initiative before He does His greatest work, because "it is he who gives you the ability to produce wealth" (Deuteronomy 8:18).

So are you tired of feeling like money just disappears from your wallet? Did your last credit card statement almost send you into cardiac arrest? If so—and if you're ready to actually *do something* about it—this chapter contains the absolute bare minimum you need to know. If you ignore everything else in this book, these first few (small) steps will help you get closer to your goals. You'll need to put forth some effort, but it's not as hard or as painful as you might think.

Here's the least you need to do:

1. Figure out what your current financial status is (net worth and debt-to-income ratio).
2. Track what you're making and spending.
3. Set limits for your future spending (budget).
4. Develop goals for your future (planning).

There you have it. 1-2-3-4, and you're off to a better financial future. Now, let's get started.

I don't have much to start with. Why do I need to think about money management and financial planning?

You may not realize it, but you've answered your own question. Why should you think about money management and financial planning? *Because you don't have much to start with.* The only way you'll ever have more than what you have right now is to use what you've got in a smarter way. Wealth and financial stability usually don't appear overnight. Yes, a few folks start out with tons of money, but the majority of us have to work hard to make ends meet.

You might feel like you're climbing a slippery slope and your paychecks just don't seem to be making much progress up the hill. You might even be slipping backwards, sucked down by rising expenses. But there's good news! Wise financial management and planning can break the cycle and increase your wealth over time—even if you're starting out with very little. But if you never take time to explore your options, you'll never know what's out there that could make an incredible difference in the future for you or your family. When you've got a plan and you're keeping more of your income, it's easier to take advantage of wealth-building opportunities that come along.

What is "net worth," and how do I calculate mine?

Net worth is simply *what you own* minus *what you owe*. Let's say you own assets like houses, cars, or other valuables with a combined total value of $100,000. However, you owe the bank $40,000 for your house, you borrowed $10,000 for your last vacation, and you've racked up $15,000 in credit card bills. Your net worth is $35,000 ($100,000 − $65,000 = $35,000).

How do you increase your net worth? By building your assets (for example, through investments) and getting rid of your debts. As you make these types of adjustments, your net worth will change over time. It's important to calculate your net worth on a regular basis, at least once a year, so you can see whether or not it's improving. Knowing your net worth will also help you make decisions with your money so you can get closer to your goals.

So what *is* your net worth today—at this very moment? Let's find out.

What You Own

Start by making a list of everything you own and establishing an honest value for each item. In other words, if you own a home, don't use the price at which you'd like to sell it; use the actual amount for which you could sell it today, without making any improvements. Go through the same exercise with your other assets—personal property, automobiles, stocks, bonds, mutual funds, IRA accounts, CDs, savings accounts, whole life insurance policies with cash value, trust funds, rental property, and anything else that has value.

Use Section A-1 of Worksheet A to document the value of all your assets, or make your own list using the worksheet as a guide. You may also want to enter these figures into an electronic spreadsheet. One benefit of doing this on a computer is that you can change the numbers in the future and easily calculate the new totals without having to do the arithmetic by hand. You can calculate net worth for you as an individual, or you can combine assets to calculate net worth for a couple. However, if you have separate property and expenses, experts recommend that you do this separately for each individual wage earner in your family.

What You Owe

Wow! Are you impressed with your total assets? That's good, but it's not the whole picture. Your assets count towards what's called your "gross net worth"—that is, what you're worth before subtracting out what you owe. Now it's time to see what parts of your assets actually belong to someone else. Let's look at your debts.

Use Section A-2 of Worksheet A to establish what you owe. Include mortgages, car loans, school loans, financing for your furniture, credit card balances, installment loans, and every type of debt that will have to be repaid. Use the total owed rather than the monthly payments; monthly payments matter for your budget, but total debt is what's important in figuring your net worth.

Also, order a copy of your credit report. You're entitled to one free report every year (visit www.annualcreditreport.com). This shows what the financial world believes you owe. Go through everything to make sure the information is accurate. If you find errors, contact the credit bureaus directly to dispute the amount (www.equifax.com, www.experian.com, www.tuc.com) so the errors can be corrected.

Your Net Worth

Now, subtract your debts from your assets using Section A-3 of Worksheet A and you'll be staring your net worth in the face. If you look at the numbers and find them utterly depressing, don't crumple up the paper and chuck the entire process. You have to consider your situation as an opportunity rather than a problem. Now that you've done this work, it can help you make meaningful life changes to improve your situation. For instance, you may need to develop a plan to reduce your debt, or you might need to acquire more assets by purchasing a home, making investments, or committing to save more of your income each month. A budget and advice from your financial team can help you make these important changes.

On the other hand, if the numbers look better than you anticipated, don't think of it as a free pass to spend without limits. You could lose your good standing more quickly than you think if you take it for granted. Instead, realize that you've just taken your first step toward greater financial freedom. You're doing something right, and you need to continue improving. Your financial team can help you find ways to maximize your good situation and plan for a steady flow of passive income as you grow older.

Worksheet A: Calculating Your Net Worth

SECTION A-1: ASSETS

<u>Market Value of Owned Real Estate:</u>

Primary Residence $_____

Secondary Residence (Rental Properties, Second Homes) $_____

Land and Commercial Property $_____

<u>Personal Property:</u>

Automobiles $_____

Jewelry $_____

Household Items (such as furniture, art, antiques) $_____

Other (such as collections, heirlooms) $_____

<u>Other:</u>

Cash (loose cash, checking account balance, piggy bank cash) $_____

Savings Account Balances (include CDs, money market accounts) $_____

Stocks and Bonds (present market value) $_____

Life Insurance (cash value) $_____

IRA accounts $_____

401(k) and other Retirement/Pension Funds $_____

Trusts $_____

Other $_____

Total Personal Assets $_____

SECTION A-2: DEBTS

Real Estate Mortgages and Equity Loans on Real Estate Property:

Primary Residence $_____

Secondary Residence $_____

Land and Commercial $_____

Personal Property Debt:

Automobiles $_____

Financing on Household Items (such as furniture, electronics) $_____

Other Personal Property Debt $_____

Other:

School Loans $_____

Business Loans $_____

Credit Card Debt $_____

Personal Debt to Friends/Relatives $_____

Past Due Bills (such as medical, utilities) $_____

Other Loans or Debt $_____

Total Personal Debt $_____

SECTION A-3: NET WORTH

Total Assets – Total Debt = Net Worth: $_____

Do I really have to track what I make and what I spend?

Only if you want to improve your financial situation. If you don't know how you're using your money now, it's hard to see where you can improve. It's like asking your doctor to diagnose and heal you without ever being able to examine your symptoms. When you do some tracking and then look back at how much you make and where it goes each month, you can finally see if there are "viruses" in your spending habits. You may discover that you have a weak financial immune system, and you'd be in serious trouble in a hurry if tragedy struck unexpectedly.

Now you may be thinking, *Receipts and papers and bills, oh my!* Don't worry. Your closet or drawer of financial records doesn't have to be as scary as the dark forest in *The Wizard of Oz*. It might take some time to get everything organized, but you'll be glad when you realize the powerful impact budgeting can have on your financial future. So pull out that bill file, dig around for those old income tax returns, and go through those drawers and closets where you've been stashing your financial history for years. Grab all the information you can find. It might take a day or two. Or you can work on this project one or two hours a day for several days. The important thing is doing it, not how long it takes.

As you work to identify all your income and expenses, create some order out of your information chaos by filing or storing your documents in a system that makes sense to you. When you're finished, you'll have a bonus prize—the basis for your financial files in the future. You'll never have to start from scratch again!

How do I figure out what I'm making and what I'm spending?

When you've got all your past financial records available (tax returns, old bills, receipts, and credit card statements), use Worksheet B to record your average monthly totals for each income and expense category. You can do this in several ways. One approach is to make thirteen copies of Worksheet

B and fill out one for each month (or use your own paper for monthly to-tals). Then calculate your monthly averages on the last copy. That's the best way to go. The more realistic method for many people is to calculate income and expenses only twice, once for your most expensive month and once for your least expensive month. Maybe December, during the holiday frenzy, and February, when you're stuck at home trying to figure out how to recover from the holiday frenzy. Again, a computer spreadsheet can be formatted like Worksheet B.

Regardless of the method you choose, the important thing is that you end up with an honest and accurate dollar amount. (For those of you who hated math in school and have purposely forgotten those painful lessons, you can calculate your yearly average for a particular category by adding all monthly totals for that category, and then dividing that grand total by 12.)

WORKSHEET B—TRACKING YOUR INCOME AND SPENDING

MONTH: _____ *(OR WRITE "YEARLY AVERAGE")*

SECTION B-1: MY INCOME

Gross Salary, Wages, Tips, or Commissions $_____

(before taxes, insurance, and other deductions)

Income from Rental Property $_____

Dividends and Interest Income $_____

(from investments, savings accounts, CDs, money markets, etc.)

Money from Trusts, Pension Funds, Retirement Accounts, or Other Savings

$_____

Payments received for Alimony or Child Support $_____

Other Income $_____

Total Gross Income *(per month)* $_____

SECTION B-2: MY TAXES
(amounts withheld or paid out of salary, wages, and commissions)

Federal Taxes $_____

State Taxes $_____

Social Security Deductions $_____

Local Taxes $_____

Medicare deductions *(if applicable)* $_____

Total Taxes *(per month)* $_____

SECTION B-3: MY SPENDING

<u>Housing-Related Expenses</u>

Mortgage Payment $_____

(may include taxes and home insurance)

Utilities: Power *(such as electric, gas, fuel)* $_____

Utilities: Water and Sewage $_____

Utilities: Waste Management $_____

Rent Payment $_____

Property Taxes (if not included in mortgage payment) $_____

Condo or Homeowners Association Fees $_____

Homeowners or Renters Insurance $_____

(if not included in mortgage payment)

Maintenance Expenses *(such as home repair, improvements)* $_____

Phone Service *(in-home line)* $_____

Cell Phones $_____

Internet $_____

Cable or Satellite Television $_____

Lawn Care Service/Landscaping $_____

Cleaning Service $_____

Termite/Pest Control Service $_____

Total House-Related Expenses $_____

<u>Transportation Expenses</u>

Car Payment $_____

Automobile Insurance $_____

Gas and Oil $_____

Maintenance and Repair $_____

Parking Fees $_____

Road Tolls and Bridge Fees $_____

Public Transportation Costs *(such as Fares, Passes)* $_____

Total Transportation Expenses $_____

Insurance Premiums

Health/Dental Insurance $_____

Disability Insurance $_____

Life Insurance $_____

Other Insurance $_____

Total Insurance Expenses $_____

Personal Care and Hygiene Expenses

Clothing $_____

Hair Care $_____

Laundry and Dry Cleaning *(if not done at home)* $_____

Nail Care and Cosmetics $_____

Other $_____

Total Personal Care/Hygiene Expenses $_____

<u>Food Expenses</u>

Groceries $_____

(include all items regularly bought at the grocery store, including paper products, personal hygiene products, laundry and cleaning supplies)

Eating Out $_____

(include trips to restaurants, fast food, convenience stores)

Other $_____

Total Food Expenses $_____

<u>Medical Expenses *(include costs for children, if applicable)*</u>

Insurance Deductibles *(and other bills not covered by insurance)* $_____

Doctor Visit Payments *(if applicable)* $_____

Prescription Drug Costs $_____

Medications Bought Over-the-Counter $_____

Other $_____

Total Medical Expenses $_____

<u>Caring for My Children</u>

School Tuition Fees $_____

Activity Expenses *(such as field trips, sports, music lessons)* $_____

Clothing and Uniforms $_____

Gifts $_____

Child Support Payments and Child Care Costs $_____

Other Expenses $_____

Total Spending for My Children $_____

Entertainment and "Extras"

Vacations $_____

Health Club or Personal Fitness $_____

Hobbies $_____

Movies, Social Events, Theatre, Dates, etc. $_____

Books, Magazines, and Music $_____

Clubs, Associations, or Other Group Expenses $_____

Other $_____

Total Entertainment/Extras Expenses $_____

"Misfit" Expenses *(things that don't fall into other categories)*

Debt Payments for Loans *(if not already included above)* $_____

Charitable Donations $_____

"Fudge Factor"—For Things I Might Have Forgotten $_____

Total Misfit Expenses $_____

SECTION B-4: ADDING IT ALL UP (PER MONTH)

<u>My Current Spending Limit</u>

Income Remaining After Taxes $_____

(total gross income minus total taxes)

<u>My Spending Habits</u>

Total Housing Expenses $_____

Total Transportation Expenses $_____

Total Insurance Expenses $_____

Total Personal Care and Hygiene Expenses $_____

Total Food Expenses $_____

Total Medical Expenses $_____

Total Spending for My Children $_____

Total Entertainment/Extras Spending $_____

Total Misfit Expenses $_____

Total Expenses $_____

WHAT I HAVE TO WORK WITH:

Money I Can Save or Invest to Reach My Financial Goals $_____

(Subtract total expenses from income remaining after taxes.)

What good does a budget do?

Setting a budget helps you control your expenses and may even make you feel better about your financial condition. By experimenting with your budget figures on paper, you can make wiser decisions about whether or not you can afford a large purchase without creating a financial disaster. As you adjust your budget and learn to spend within your limits, you'll also free up money to save and invest, even if your income doesn't change. With more money saved and invested, you're better prepared for life's financial surprises, little and large.

After examining your spending habits, you might discover your income doesn't support your expenses. Usually it's hard to make quick changes to your income—to increase your earnings, find other sources of income, or increase your investments and savings. You can, however, have a quick and decisive impact on your spending. Lowering expenses can make a big difference at this stage of your money education. Overall, if you spend less, decrease your debt, and increase your savings and investments, you get to keep more of your money. The money you can keep can be put to work for your future.

How do I create a budget?

To establish your budget, use Worksheet C and record your average monthly expenses (from Worksheet B) for each category in the first column. Then go through your expenses and decide on realistic spending limits for each category. Put these new limits in the second column on Worksheet C.

Some of your expenses are fixed and can't be changed; for instance, your health insurance might have to stay the same. But think carefully about where you *could* reduce your spending; those are the categories in which you can set lower limits. You might not need five cell phones in your family right now; perhaps you can reduce it to just two. Or perhaps you can exercise self-control and avoid buying new clothes unless absolutely necessary.

Your budget will be unique to *your* situation, but challenge yourself to reduce your spending. However, don't be so ambitious that you fill the final column with unrealistic numbers you'll never be able to meet. Keep in mind that in some areas you may even need to increase your spending where it will help toward your overall goals.

When you're taking a good hard look at your spending, it's also important to consider the difference between needs, wants, and desires.

- *Needs* are basic requirements, such as food, clothing, shelter, and medical coverage.
- *Wants* involve choices about the quality of goods you buy. For instance, will you purchase fun clothes or work clothes? Eat steak or hamburger? Buy a new car or a used car?
- *Desires* go above and beyond wants and can be purchased only out of what's left over when all other obligations have been met. Vacations, personal luxuries, and extra toys or gadgets would all be classified as desires.

When you think you've set reasonable limits for each spending category, add up your new budget figures (second column). Is this total less than your previous total monthly expenses (first column)? If so, you've reduced your spending and taken a huge step toward meeting your financial goals.

Now, subtract your new total spending budget (second column) from your Total Monthly Income (after taxes) that you calculated earlier on Worksheet B. The number you get represents the cash you'll have left over in your wallet or bank account each month if you follow your new budget. You can save or invest this extra cash to increase your net worth and your financial strength for the future. It can also serve as a cushion for emergencies.

Now that you've created a budget, stick to your plan by tracking your monthly expenses and keeping a close eye on how close you're coming to your budget limits. Try hard not to go over your limits unless you just don't have another option. Guard carefully against complacency or lack of commitment. Creating a budget is the easy part; the challenge lies in sustaining the self-discipline to stick to it and not fall prey to your wants and desires. On the other hand, you also need to be flexible and realistic. At times you may have to exceed your budget. And if your spending goes out of control, don't worry. Just recommit to your budget as soon as you can.

If you're part of a family, following the budget will require the cooperation of every family member who spends household funds, so get everyone involved. You might even want to reward yourself or your family after a long period of success with your new budget. You can stash away some of your extra cash each month and use it for a family vacation, a special activity, or special gifts for each other.

WORKSHEET C: MY NEW BUDGET

In the first column on the next page, copy the totals from Worksheet B above where you tracked your spending. In the second column, record *your new spending limit* for each item.

HOUSING-RELATED EXPENSES

Mortgage Payment (before: $_____)   NEW LIMIT: $_____

Utilities: Power (before: $_____)   NEW LIMIT: $_____

Utilities: Water and Sewage (before: $_____)   NEW LIMIT: $_____

Utilities: Waste Management (before: $_____)   NEW LIMIT: $_____

Rent Payment (before: $_____)   NEW LIMIT: $_____

Property Taxes (before: $_____)   NEW LIMIT: $_____

Condo or Homeowners Assoc. Fees (before: $_____)   NEW LIMIT: $_____

Homeowners or Renters Insurance (before: $_____)   NEW LIMIT: $_____

Maintenance Expenses (before: $_____)   NEW LIMIT: $_____

Phone Service (before: $_____)   NEW LIMIT: $_____

Cell Phones (before: $_____)   NEW LIMIT: $_____

Internet Usage (before: $_____)   NEW LIMIT: $_____

Cable or Satellite Television (before: $_____)   NEW LIMIT: $_____

Lawn Care Service/Landscaping (before: $_____)   NEW LIMIT: $_____

Cleaning Service (before: $_____)   NEW LIMIT: $_____

Termite/Pest Control Service (before: $_____)   NEW LIMIT: $_____

Housing Total (before: $_____)   NEW LIMIT: $_____

TRANSPORTATION EXPENSES

Car Payment (before: $_____)   NEW LIMIT: $_____

Automobile Insurance (before: $_____)   NEW LIMIT: $_____

Gas and Oil (before: $_____)   NEW LIMIT: $_____

Maintenance and Repair Expenses (before: $_____)   NEW LIMIT: $_____

Parking Fees (before: $_____)   NEW LIMIT: $_____

Road Tolls and Bridge Fees (before: $_____)   NEW LIMIT: $_____

Public Transportation Costs (before: $_____)   NEW LIMIT: $_____

Transportation Total (before: $_____)   NEW LIMIT: $_____

INSURANCE PREMIUMS

Health/Dental Insurance (before: $_____)   NEW LIMIT: $_____

Disability Insurance (before: $_____)   NEW LIMIT: $_____

Life Insurance (before: $_____)   NEW LIMIT: $_____

Other Insurance (before: $_____)   NEW LIMIT: $_____

Insurance Total (before: $_____)   NEW LIMIT: $_____

PERSONAL CARE AND HYGIENE EXPENSES

Clothing (before: $_____)   NEW LIMIT: $_____

Hair Care (before: $_____)   NEW LIMIT: $_____

Laundry and Dry Cleaning (before: $_____)   NEW LIMIT: $_____

Nail Care and Cosmetics (before: $_____)   NEW LIMIT: $_____

Other (before: $_____)   NEW LIMIT: $_____

Personal Care/Hygiene Total (before: $_____)   NEW LIMIT: $_____

FOOD EXPENSES

Groceries (before: $_____)   NEW LIMIT: $_____

Eating Out (before: $_____)   NEW LIMIT: $_____

Other (before: $_____)   NEW LIMIT: $_____

Food Total (before: $_____)   NEW LIMIT: $_____

MEDICAL EXPENSES

Insurance Deductibles (before: $_____)   NEW LIMIT: $_____

Doctor Visit Payments (before: $_____)   NEW LIMIT: $_____

Prescription Drug Costs (before: $_____)   NEW LIMIT: $_____

Over-the-Counter Medications (before: $_____)   NEW LIMIT: $_____

Other (before: $_____)   NEW LIMIT: $_____

Medical Total (before: $_____)   NEW LIMIT: $_____

CARING FOR MY CHILDREN

School Tuition Fees (before: $_____)   NEW LIMIT: $_____

Activity Expenses (before: $_____)   NEW LIMIT: $_____

Clothing and Uniforms (before: $_____)   NEW LIMIT: $_____

Gifts (before: $_____)   NEW LIMIT: $_____

Child Support and Child Care (before: $_____)   NEW LIMIT: $_____

Other Expenses (before: $_____)   NEW LIMIT: $_____

Spending for Children Total (before: $_____)   NEW LIMIT: $_____

ENTERTAINMENT AND "EXTRAS"

Vacations (before: $_____)   NEW LIMIT: $_____

Health Club or Personal Fitness (before: $_____)   NEW LIMIT: $_____

Hobbies (before: $_____)   NEW LIMIT: $_____

Movies, Social Events, Theatre, Dates, etc. (before: $_____)   NEW LIMIT: $_____

Books, Magazines, and Music (before: $_____)   NEW LIMIT: $_____

Clubs, Associations, or Other Group Fees (before: $_____)   NEW LIMIT: $_____

Other (before: $_____)   NEW LIMIT: $_____

Entertainment/Extras Total (before: $_____)   NEW LIMIT: $_____

"MISFIT" EXPENSES

Debt Payments for Loans (before: $_____)   NEW LIMIT: $_____

Charitable Donations (before: $_____)   NEW LIMIT: $_____

"Fudge Factor" (before: $_____)   NEW LIMIT: $_____

Misfit Total (before: $_____)   NEW LIMIT: $_____

Now for your budget's real bottom line, add the totals from each area:

Housing (before: $_____)   NEW LIMIT: $_____

Transportation (before: $_____)   NEW LIMIT: $_____

Insurance (before: $_____)   NEW LIMIT: $_____

Personal Care/Hygiene (before: $_____)   NEW LIMIT: $_____

Food (before: $_____)   NEW LIMIT: $_____

Medical (before: $_____)   NEW LIMIT: $_____

Spending for Children (before: $_____)   NEW LIMIT: $_____

Entertainment/Extras (before: $_____)   NEW LIMIT: $_____

Misfit (before: $_____)   NEW LIMIT: $_____

Budget Total (before: $_____)   NEW LIMIT: $_____

How much debt should I have?

First, calculate your debt-to-income ratio. To do this, use the table below to determine your total monthly outlay for debt payments.

Debt Category

Housing Debt (mortgage or rent) $_____

Loan Payments $_____

Equity Lines of Credit Payments $_____

Revolving Credit Payments (financing on furniture or appliances) $_____

Credit Card Payments (minimum monthly payment) $_____

Alimony/Child Support $_____

Other Monthly Debt Payments $_____

Total Monthly Debt Load $_____

Now, divide your Total Monthly Debt Load by your Total Monthly Income (after taxes) that you calculated on Worksheet B. The resulting percent is your debt-to-income ratio. Lenders use this ratio to determine how much they can allow you to borrow, and you can use this ratio to examine whether you're too far in debt. The idea is that the higher your ratio, the harder it will be for you to make your payments out of your current income. While every situation is different, general rules about debt-to-income ratios include the following:

- 40 percent or more means your credit situation is out of control. You need to take immediate action or you may crash and burn.
- 36 to 40 percent puts you in the borderline category. You may be approved for more credit, but paying the bills on time will be a struggle.
- 30 to 36 percent is okay. Lenders should have no problem loaning you money, but you're still not in the best possible position.
- Under 30 percent—You're doing well, but you need to watch your other expenses so you can maintain this low level of debt.

I have a hard time knowing exactly what I want from my life, let alone how to get there. Why is it so important to have written goals for my future?

The Bible teaches us, "Know where you are headed, and you will stay on solid ground" (Proverbs 4:26, CEV). If you were going to spend a year at sea on a boat, it would take planning. So would building a sports team or running for public office. Almost everything worthwhile requires some level of planning; achieving financial success is no different. You need specific goals, and a plan for achieving them. If you aim at nothing, you'll likely end up nowhere with nothing. Do you really want to allow chance or other people to dictate your financial future? Do you want to passively accept what the world throws at you and pretend you can't change a thing? You might find yourself up the proverbial creek without a proverbial paddle. Don't leave yourself vulnerable when it's in your power to make a difference!

Now, even if you've got a steel trap for a mind, life makes it tough to remember, work towards, and achieve your goals if they're not written down. Financial goals written on paper are always more real than those that stay in your head. Written goals have a way of feeling "official" and undeniable. They're harder to rationalize away. And written goals are easier to modify and refer back to when things get tough. So get out another sheet of paper and get ready to make some plans.

When will I finally reach my goals?

Different goals require different time periods. You might reach some goals in weeks or months, and others might take years. Some goals depend on your achieving other goals first. For instance, a long-term retirement goal might depend upon a mid-term investment goal. For most of us, our goals fluctuate from time to time, as priorities and conditions change. For that reason, it's usually better to establish short-term, mid-term, and long-term objectives. And you need to remain flexible.

Talk to me more about short-term, mid-term, and long-term goals.

Long-term objectives don't generally change as circumstances change, and they focus on our desire for financial security, a comfortable retirement, or enough wealth and passive income that money is no longer a concern. Or maybe you're planning for your children's education; it's not too early to do this when they're still infants. These goals for the distant future need to be realistic, but they can also be ambitious—particularly if you're setting them early in life. Bear in mind that meeting long-term financial objectives takes discipline. If you dip into long-term funds, you may miss your goals. Take your long-term objectives seriously.

Each person has to determine her time frame for mid-term objectives, but these are typically three to ten years in the future. This category might include saving for a down payment on a house or condo, for an advanced degree, for a child's private school tuition, for a fabulous vacation, or for a new car. Mid-term goals might also include investments, with an eye toward a target net worth or a specific amount of money in mutual funds or IRAs. Paying off car loans, equity lines of credit, or other debt might be among your mid-term goals. Mid-term objectives often change as your situation does—think weddings, babies, and unexpected financial needs. Usually these goals require substantial amounts of money, but not so much that it's impossible to save what you need. *Saving* for mid-term goals is a wiser choice than paying for them on credit and increasing your debt load.

Short-term objectives are usually "where the action is" (and the pitfalls). These are goals between one and three years out into the future, and they might include paying off credit card debt; retiring an automobile loan or being in a position to take one on; or taking on a home improvement project.

Obviously, your current financial situation—your assets and liabilities—will determine where specific financial objectives fall along your timeline. Here are several guidelines for establishing your goals:

- Write your goals down on paper (or on your computer) in a form that you can easily reference.
- Be realistic. Don't make your goals so far-fetched you can never hope to achieve them. For example, if you take home $2000 a month after taxes, and you have regularly occurring expenses of $1400, you can't realistically expect to be a millionaire in ten years without some major changes. If you don't choose attainable goals, you'll get so frustrated you might give up on the whole process and never achieve financial success.

- Try not to overwhelm yourself. As a rule, state no more than five objectives for each time frame (short-term, mid-term, and long-term).
- Review your financial objectives every three months and see if they're still relevant.
- When circumstances change, make a trip to the financial file and evaluate the impact on your goals. A pay raise might mean pushing a goal's time frame up, since you can pay off more debt earlier or save more toward the future. On the flipside, major dental work might require moving a car purchase back a few months or a year.
- Don't throw away goals that change. A turn of events may allow you to add an objective back into your plan.
- Dream big! While you want to stay realistic, you also need to give yourself the freedom to plan for an exciting future. Some or all of your dreams could actually come true.
- Remember to choose some fun goals, if possible.

Some possibilities to consider for short-term goals:

- Reduce your debt by 20 percent.
- Increase your savings by 20 percent.
- Save enough for a year of a child's private school tuition.
- Pay off a high-interest credit card.
- Save enough to pay for a wedding.

Some goals to consider for mid-term time frames:

- Save enough for a house down payment.
- Put enough money in an accessible account for a ninety-day emergency cushion—and never tap it for regular expenses.

Some possible long-term objectives:

- Pay off a house mortgage early.
- Become debt-free.
- Invest for adequate passive retirement income.

Where else can I find information on budgeting and financial planning?

In the information age, good resources are only a click away. If you're not computer literate, public libraries or bookstores offer numerous resources. Many credit unions have brochures on the subject, too.

Some helpful websites include the following:

www.crown.org—Crown Financial Ministries offers a wealth of biblically based information to help you with money.

www.usatoday.com—The money section has a menu item for personal wealth, with useful tools and information.

www.money.com—The official site for Money magazine.

www.consumerreports.org—This site offers articles on purchasing and finances and, if you subscribe, you can get comprehensive evaluations of most products for purchase.

www.about.com—A great source of articles about financial planning and money management.

www.experian.com—One of three credit reporting firms. This site also carries some good articles and advice.

CHAPTER TWO

Victory over Stumbling Blocks

"For I know the plans I have for you," says the Lord,
"'plans for well-being and not for trouble, to give you a future and a hope."
JEREMIAH 29:11, NLV

There's truth to the old adage, "Expect the unexpected." Wouldn't it be wonderful if we could guarantee the resources to weather every financial storm in our lives? That may be impossible, but there are ways to minimize an emergency's financial impact.

The rule of thumb is always to have available at least three months' living expenses. That is the bare minimum. A cushion of six months to a year is far more desirable. For most of us, saving that much money is difficult. And it's tough to leave the money untouched when it's so accessible and there are so many wonderful things out there to do and buy.

So if you're serious about preparing for the unexpected, put the money in a separate account and consider it hands off, no matter how appealing the opportunity to spend. Consider a money market account, where your money can earn a small return.

If you find yourself struggling to save away a portion of your income, look into setting up an auto-deduction from your checking account or direct deposit by your employer. This is what I call no-brainer savings! The advent of on-line banking also allows you to easily earmark a set dollar amount to be transferred to savings on a regular basis. Eventually, you'll learn to live without the extra twenty, fifty, or one hundred dollars, and you'll probably forget about it completely. You may not be able to accumulate three months' worth of cash in a short time, but it should be among your short- or mid-term goals, ahead of that snazzy new car or that luxury cruise to Tahiti.

For many of us the biggest obstacle to saving comes from those smaller daily expenses that can add up quickly. Simple purchases, like a daily four-dollar latte, or buying lunch instead of bringing food from home, create a slow leak in your budget. Before long you're dipping into your overdraft protection on your ATM card or lowering your monthly credit card payments to fill in holes created by excessive daily spending.

Go back to your monthly spending chart. Now that you know the minimum it costs to maintain your lifestyle, take that number and multiply it by three. This is your target emergency fund balance. Remember, this cushion may have to last even longer than three months.

Ask yourself if this three-month total is really enough for meeting your needs without creating more stress on top of that caused by the hypothetical future emergency. You might be wise to think of ways to earn extra spending money on the side. For example, do you have a specific skill you can use to make money from home? If so, electronic classifieds like www.craigslist.org, ifreelance.com, and www.guru.com post a number of part-time projects for telecommuters. You might also consider picking up a part-time job in the evening or on weekends.

However, before doing this, examine your budget again for any other "luxuries" you can reasonably do without. For instance, consider canceling your cable and switching to a monthly on-line DVD rental service, which can be as low as ten dollars a month. Ask yourself if you absolutely need a DSL connection, landline, and cell phone. Consolidating bills and eliminating nonessential services can free up enough money to eliminate the need to moonlight. And, although you might not believe it right now, many of these extras won't seem as critical to you once you've had the opportunity to watch your savings grow.

Now you're ready to set up that money market account with an automatic system for transferring money to it on a regular basis. The deposits will accumulate interest and the emergency account will grow until you need it.

What are some typical unforeseen problems that can wreck my budget?

You've planned your expenses, your budget health is good, and you're chugging along nicely. All of a sudden a surprise throws your budget health into a tailspin. Maybe it's...

A hidden debt: Many people overlook non-regular debts, such as doctor bills and family loans, and when the time comes to pay for them, you find your budget doesn't allow for them. In order to avoid such surprises, maintain a list of all debts and update it frequently. Find out if your employer offers a medical reimbursement account plan which allows you to set aside an amount tax free each pay period, exclusively for meeting medical costs like co-payments and prescriptions. Your human resources representative or benefits department can offer detailed information.

Impulse buying: Watch out for spontaneous purchases—items you hadn't planned to buy when you went shopping. (Ladies, can you relate? I know I can!) Most impulse purchases are "great deals" we hadn't expected to find. But have you ever bought an item of clothing just because it was on sale, then took another look at home and exclaimed, "What was I thinking?"

Impulse buying isn't always bad; some deals are truly too good to pass up. However, taking a little time to think about your purchase can help you better decide whether it's necessary. Be honest and ask yourself why you want it. Will it really be useful? Are you buying it because it makes you feel better? (You know...shopping therapy.) Or because you feel you deserve a reward? If the item is something you *want* rather than *need*, perhaps you should wait until you've thought about it some more.

Also, be careful what you put into your cart. If you have two similar items, compare them and keep only the one that is the better purchase. Making a list before you come to the store, and then committing to the list while shopping, can serve as a wonderful deterrent to impulsive buying. If you live in a metropolitan area, look into on-line grocery services. The delivery charges are typically within the ten-to-twenty-dollar range, which is probably less than what you might have spent on those unplanned purchases. This is also an effective strategy for parents, who are all too familiar with their children's persistent requests for the toys and candy strategically displayed throughout the store.

Overspending on gifts: We buy lots of gifts each holiday season. Then in January and February the credit card bills arrive, along with their shocking balances. We spend the next nine months paying off those charges. By September, most of us are relieved it's all behind us. Then Thanksgiving comes, and the cycle begins anew.

If that sounds familiar, join the club. A major budget-buster in most families is overspending on gifts. To bring the cost of gifts under control, consider doing the following:

1. Make a list of the people to whom you'll give gifts.

2. Next to each name, do *not* write down the item you plan to buy each person. This is a common mistake, and the biggest reason for overspending. Instead, state the dollar amount you'll spend on each person. Remember that the amount you write for each person must include the costs of holiday cards, wrapping paper and attendant supplies (such as ribbons, boxes, and tape), and taxes and shipping costs for out-of-town recipients.

3. When you've finished, total up the individual amounts.

4. If the total is more than you want or can afford to spend, cut the list by removing names, reducing the amount per name, or both. Then calculate the new total.

5. When you settle on a final total, go to the bank and withdraw that amount in cash. If you're uncomfortable carrying lots of cash, get traveler's checks. If you don't have this amount in the bank, your total is more than you can afford. Repeat step 4.

6. With a new total—and the requisite cash in hand—you're ready to head for the stores. But before you go, remove from your wallet or purse all your check books, debit cards, ATM cards, and credit cards. Leave them all at home!

7. Shop through your list. Remember: You've got a limited amount of cash, so if you overspend on one person, you'll be forced to underspend on another. When you're out of money, you're done!

Not only does this strategy prevent you from overspending, it also enables you to enjoy the holiday season debt-free. What an enjoyable way to start the New Year!

How do I know if I'm in serious debt trouble?

If you're in debt trouble, you know it when the bills come in and you're sitting at the table, head in hands, trying to figure out how you're going to pay them all. There are many signs—some obvious, some more subtle—that you have a major debt problem and need to solve it ASAP. Here are some of them:

- Someone has denied you credit.
- You bounce checks.
- You screen phone calls because creditors and collectors are calling.
- You're using one credit card to pay another credit card bill.
- You have more than two or three major credit cards, and you use them all.
- After paying your credit card bill, you find yourself charging the same amount in new purchases or cash advances the following month, creating a vicious cycle.
- You've been known to hide your credit card statement from your spouse or other family member.
- You take out cash advances (bad idea) to pay other bills or make it until payday.
- You've tried to purchase something on your credit card and have been declined.
- You have no savings.
- You need to use credit cards to pay for necessities like groceries and fuel.

If you see yourself in this picture, there's help. Spread out those credit card bills on a table and make a pledge to pay them down, starting with those carrying the highest interest rates. Get rid of multiple credit cards as quickly as you can. Use only cash to pay for items like food, fuel, entertainment, clothing, shoes, and toiletries. If you don't have the cash, buy less.

Doing without is never easy. Seeking advice and support from people in the same situation can help you stay focused and motivated. The Motley Fool (www.fool.com) website is a highly regarded, reputable source of information on personal finance and investing.

If you still cannot get out of this hole, talk to your creditors about a payoff plan, or seek help from the Consumer Credit Counseling Service, a nonprofit agency dedicated to helping consumers manage debt. CCCS also offers credit counseling and can help you develop a budget, get practical advice, or participate in their debt management system, which allows you to pay all of your creditors with a single monthly payment.

When choosing a credit counseling agency, avoid any that want to charge you high fees. Reputable agencies are members of the National Foundation for Credit Counseling or the Association of Independent Credit Counseling Agencies. They should also be members of the Better Business Bureau. Before signing on with one, check the yellow pages and visit the Consumer Credit Counseling Service at http://www.cccsstl.org for guidance.

I shouldn't have to say this, but here it is anyway: Once you straighten out your debt mess, do whatever it takes to avoid getting into this fix again. You're the only one with the power to make this happen. Forgive yourself, be proud of your determination and discipline, and resolve to live debt-free as you go forward. I have yet to meet one person who hasn't struggled with debt at some point in life. Myself included.

How does credit work, and why do I have to deal with this?

Credit is a complex and controversial subject. If we put God in charge of our lives and our businesses, He promises to make us the lender, not the borrower—the head, not the tail (see Deuteronomy 28:12–13). Some people interpret this to mean you should never borrow, period! If that's your conviction, stick with it. But if God says it's okay to be the *lender,* it means someone has to be the borrower. For houses, vehicles, and other high-ticket items that would otherwise be out of reach, even wise consumers often find borrowing necessary.

Past generations didn't use credit nearly as extensively. They lived by the rule, "If you can't afford it, don't buy it." But the trend today is to overextend one's resources through credit. It's always easier to run up debt than to pay it off, as many have learned the hard way. And with credit card companies soliciting even teenagers, bad credit decisions often stay with individuals for a decade or more.

A good rule of thumb is to purchase on credit only those items that will considerably outlast the length of the loan—homes, cars, educational expenses, some home improvements, and other large-ticket items of lasting value. If you don't need to use credit for things such as food, fuel, and utilities, then don't. It's too easy to run up a balance, even in a month or two, and face interest charges long after the pantry needs refilling, the car needs gas, and you've switched from needing heat to air conditioning.

If you need to use credit for everyday expenses, you're probably living beyond your means. You need to get out the budget numbers to see where the money's going. Maybe your situation has changed subtly and you need to redraw your budget to meet your current needs without going into debt.

There are other times when the use of a credit card makes sense, even though the purchase won't have a particularly long life. Like when you want to track the progress of a shipped package, when you might need to dispute a charge for an on-line purchase, or when you find an amazing bargain you can pay off responsibly in one or two months. Just don't make it a habit. And, whenever possible, pay off your charges in full each month.

If you're honest with yourself about the real cost of borrowed money, you'll be more aware of the pros and cons of credit. According to a spokesperson for Experian, one of the nation's credit reporting firms, if you owe $10,000 at 18 percent, and you make the minimum payments, that debt will actually cost you $28,079 to pay off.

How is my credit score determined?

At the time of this writing, the nation's three major credit bureaus are creating a more understandable scoring system than the one that has been in use. Currently your score is reflected in a number (your FICO score, developed by Fair Isaac Corporation), but soon it will become a grade, just like in school. According to the Associated Press, the new system is called "VantageScore" and will provide a scoring model that works more consistently across the three credit bureaus. In the past, each agency used its own formulas to generate scores.

Can you explain how my credit score affects me and why I should care?

Credit organizations want your business, but their level of confidence in your ability to repay your debt is directly linked to your buying habits, income, assets, and history of repaying previous debts. Your credit score is a measure of your credit worthiness.

A huge factor impacting your ability to turn around your financial situation is this score. Almost every financial decision you make in your life is linked to your credit score. So it's important to understand how it's calculated, how it's used, and how you can improve it. FICO scores determine everything from the interest rate on your credit cards to the interest rate on your mortgage. A good score can get you the best interest rates and deals, whereas a low score means paying high interest rates and at times may even disqualify you for a loan or a credit card.

What is my FICO score based on?

While your credit score is becoming more understandable, Jean Ann Fox, director of consumer protection with the nonprofit Consumer Federation of America, says "It's a new recipe, but the same old ingredients."[1]

According to Fair Isaac, these are the most important factors, including the "weight" (percent of your score) each one contributes to the calculation:

1. Previous Payment History: 35 percent

- Trade line information specific to payment history.
- Collections, public records, judgments, and liens.
- Severity, recentness, and frequency of delinquencies. (For example, a recent late payment on a mortgage can result in a fifty-point loss in one's credit score.)

Payment history includes both currently open accounts and accounts that have been closed.

2. Outstanding Debt: 30 percent

- Relationship between total balances and credit limits. (High credit limits show that a person could potentially go into that much more debt, thus being a higher risk. But if you use only a small amount of your available credit, you're a lower risk. Your credit balance should *not* exceed 34 percent of your credit limit. Don't max out your credit cards.)
- Number of balances across all trade lines. (Having multiple accounts open increases your credit limits and creates a higher risk.)

3. Credit History: 15 percent

- How long credit has been in use. (The older an item of derogatory credit is, the less it reflects in your score.)

4. Pursuit of New Credit: 5 percent

- Number of inquiries. (Recent credit checks can weigh down your score, although the repositories have begun to recognize that people often aggressively shop around for mortgages and automobile loans. Credit score models have changed so that multiple inquiries within a fourteen-day period are counted as one, although all the inquiries will show on the credit file. Inquiries that don't show up in your credit score are those from account management/account review; promotional inquiries; potential employer inquiries; and medical/ health inquiries.)
- Amount of time since the last inquiry.
- Number of new accounts opened in the past year.

5. Types of Credit in Use: 15 percent

- Types of credit include installment loans, revolving accounts (including overdraft protection), and debit accounts.

What is a good FICO score?

A FICO score is a three-digit number ranging between 300 and 850. If you have a score below 500, few if any businesses will lend you money—not without attaching your firstborn to the business terms. A score below 600 is considered poor. Scores above 720 are considered "good credit." Your goal should be to keep your score between 720 and 850. You'll get the same interest rate on a loan with any score in that range.

What should I do when I've been denied a loan?

Request a copy of your credit report and a reason for the denial. Work immediately to send dispute letters on any items that aren't valid. If you can pay off any of the debt, especially the small amounts, this will help. Pay loans and credit cards down to below 30 percent of available credit, if possible. Also try to set up a payment plan with creditors and have this noted on your accounts. If you research other loan options, tell them your credit score and ask what they can do for you without running another report. You don't want yet another inquiry on your report to negatively affect your credit score.

How can I clear up any derogatory statements on my credit report?

Negotiate with collectors and businesses to remove any late payments or collections from a credit report. Often collectors will happily remove notices in exchange for prompt payment. This works best when the credit branch of the business is closely connected to the sales branch, and when you're a significant customer.

Also be aware of the statute of limitations on any debt you're attempting to clear by dispute. The statute of limitations is a period of time, set by state law, within which a creditor may file a lawsuit to enforce its legal rights. Once the period of the statute has "run," the creditor can no longer sue on the account.

If you have federal student loans that fell into default, pursue loan "rehabilitation." Labels of "collection" or "default" will be removed from a loan's history with regular payments over the course of a year. Keep an eye on the way student loans are reported. Student loans are notorious for being reported multiple times, making it look like your monthly payment obligations are higher than they actually are.

What else can I do to improve my credit score?

Your most important strategy is to regularly check your credit report.

1. Get your free annual report by visiting www.annualcreditreport.com.

2. Find any inaccuracies in your reports. Check all information, not just information marked "negative." Even incorrect neutral information may weigh negatively on your report. For example, if your credit limit is stated too low, you will appear to be using a higher percentage of your total capacity. This lowers your score.

3. Dispute these inaccuracies immediately with the creditors directly or with the bureaus. Creditors tend to have live operators, while bureaus do not.

You should also know that credit counseling and repair can work for and against you. Mortgage professionals caution that using a credit counseling service may negatively affect your credit report. But, on the other hand, if you need serious guidance, some credit repair organizations claim immense improvements in scores in short periods of time. Be warned that results aren't usually guaranteed, and watch for excess fees.

Would paying bills on time increase my FICO score?

Yep, big time! Timely payments—minimum payments, not necessarily full balances—account for 35 percent of your score. Punctuality helps in the short term, and over the course of a year, paying bills on time will increase your score by roughly thirty points.

• Payments more than thirty days late will affect your credit score. Note that a bill issued March 15 with a due date of March 31 doesn't become thirty days late until April 30. But if you have the means, pay earlier rather than later. A single late payment may result in a drop of more than twenty points.

- Collection accounts—usually those that are unpaid for at least six months—are much worse than late payments.
- Set up as many automated payments as possible. This will help avoid missed payments. Be sure to maintain sufficient funds in the bank account from which payments are drawn, and ensure that the address for each account is correct.

How important is it to manage my debt-to-credit-limit ratio?

Your debt-to-credit-limit ratio accounts for 30 percent of your FICO score, so it's very important. The "debt" in this formula is your combined balances on all your credit cards and loans. This is what you actually owe. The "credit limit" is the combined total limit of all your credit accounts. In other words, it's the damage you could potentially do, credit-wise, should you face financial disaster. The lower the ratio, the better it is. You can improve your ratio in two ways. First, you can increase your total capacity for borrowing. If limits on your credit cards are increased while your balances stay the same, the ratio drops and your FICO score increases. If possible, try to increase limits without triggering credit checks, which can hurt your score. And second, of course, you can improve your ratio by decreasing your total debt, paying down your balances.

Here are a few more pointers:

- Maintain good relationships with banks and other businesses. Banks will often remove late notations for valued customers. When a consumer is turned down for credit cards elsewhere, a bank will often provide a low-limit credit card. This card will increase your borrowing capacity, even if only by a small amount, and help you build a solid credit history.

- Consider secured credit cards, which factor into credit scores the same way unsecured cards do. If you open a $1000 secured credit account, it will appear in the resulting credit report that someone has trusted you enough to extend you credit, increasing your borrowing capacity by $1000.
- Pay down all of your balances. It may make sense to move balances between cards so no single balance is at more than 34 percent of its capacity.
- During mortgage refinances, you may want to consider moving some credit card debt to a lower-interest equity loan. Just be sure not to charge up the cards again.

What steps can I take to develop a "longer" credit history?

The longer the credit history the better, as it accounts for 15 percent of your credit score. Think twice about canceling credit cards you've had for a long time, erasing an important part of your credit history. (Moreover, canceling a card reduces your total credit limit, worsening your debt-to-credit-limit ratio.) Instead, you can take the following steps:

- When you begin making on-time rent and utility payments, this will help build your credit history and show that you can be trusted to pay your bills on time. Rent and utility payments are factored into your credit score as nontraditional credit and show up on your report only if you don't pay your bills on time (become delinquent).
- Build solid relationships with banks and other businesses. Banks will often extend credit cards to their customers, even with less-than-perfect credit. Many businesses like Home Depot offer financing plans that don't require clean credit.
- When buying a car, even if you don't need a loan, consider taking a small fraction of the car's cost out as a loan. Loans like these are

secured by the car itself, so in the event of failure to repay, the financing company won't suffer much loss. Repay this as soon as possible to establish good credit. This shows that you can take out a loan and be trusted to pay it off in full.

- Try to maintain at least a minimal amount of credit activity, paying off balances in full each month. It's been shown that consumers who maintain a minimal amount of credit are less likely to default on a new account than consumers who don't maintain credit.

What is a healthy credit mix?

Try to keep a variety of types of credit—major credit cards, retail cards, and installment loans like car loans and home mortgages. Your ability to handle different kinds of credit improves your credit worthiness. But remember, applying for too many credit cards and loans at once is not considered a good sign by lenders.

How can I get the best interest rate on my credit card?

Credit card companies count on the fact that most customers do not realize the importance of interest rates. Our ignorance earns them billions of dollars. First check the interest rate on your existing credit card. If you have a good credit score and a steady source of income and are still paying 15 percent or more on interest, something is wrong. You need to shop around for a card that will give you the best APR, or call your existing company and ask them to lower your rate.

What does "APR" mean?

APR stands for "annual percentage rate," and it's an important tool for you to use when comparing lenders. It's one of the simplest ways to determine the cost of money that you're borrowing, and since every lender is required by law to use the same method for calculating it, you can compare apples with apples, rather than apples with kumquats.

APR is the total interest you would pay for borrowing the money for one year, divided by the amount borrowed. This ratio is stated as a percentage. So $100 annual interest on a $1000 loan is a 10 percent APR.

Still confused? You're not alone, but being able to define an APR isn't as important as understanding the impact that it can have on your finances. It's one of the Big Three when it comes to borrowing money (the other two are the duration of the loan and the size of the payments). Credit card companies love it when you pay only minimum monthly payments. Suppose you owe $2000 at just under 10 percent and have a minimum payment of about $40. If you make only minimum payments, you'll take about five years to pay off the loan. If, however, you increase your payment to $100 per month, you're paying that interest rate for only two years. If you can make $200 payments, it comes to less than one year. Everything that you haven't paid out in interest is money in your pocket.

When you're deciding which cards to use and which to pay off, check out the APR listed near the bottom of each month's bill. Use lower-interest cards, and pay off higher-interest cards first.

When shopping for a mortgage, be aware that comparing APRs can be complicated, as many lenders roll some fees into the mortgage. More on this in Chapter 7.

When you're shopping for any credit, ask for APR information in writing, and ask the lender to itemize everything that's included in calculating that number.

How can I save money on my credit cards?

Some money-saving methods take only some digging and a bit of creativity. So before you resign yourself to living with high-interest balances, do some research and find out whether any of these options are available to you.

If your credit is good—a check of your three credit ratings should give you the big picture—you shouldn't be paying high credit card interest. Shop rates on the Internet. "The Motley Fool" (www.fool.com) is one source of valuable advice on finding low-interest credit cards.

Don't confuse the short-term "incentive" rates, which are offered to lure you into applying for the card, with the regular rates that take effect after the honeymoon period is over. You may be married to that regular rate for a long time, so educate yourself about it before committing.

If you can obtain a low-interest credit card, it may be to your advantage to transfer high-interest balances to it, allowing you to pay them off more quickly at a lower cost to you. Be sure to weigh the cost of any balance transfer fees against your interest savings.

Once you've done this, put your "empty" high-interest card in your freezer in a plastic container filled with water. Yes, I'm serious. Put the container in the back of the freezer. Do the same with any credit cards you want to take out of commission. Hopefully you'll forget them entirely until you're ready to move to a new home and need to empty the refrigerator. If you do have a weak moment, the time required to defrost the container may allow you to rethink your decision.

If you have high credit card rates, it may be sensible to dip into your accessible savings to pay them off. This is not permission to raid your savings, clear the cards, and then start building debt again. But if you're getting 2.5 percent on your savings and have credit cards charging 15 percent, you'll save more by tapping into your savings to get rid of the interest payments.

Make the largest payment possible toward higher-interest cards while paying the minimum or a bit more on lower-interest cards. Try first to get all balances below 34 percent (for a better credit score), and then work to pay off all your cards. And won't that feel good!

Are balance transfers a good idea?

Transferring balances from credit cards with high interest rates to those with lower rates is a good thing, within reason. These days many companies are offering zero percent APR on balance transfers for six months to a year. If you happen to get such a deal, you can use it to get rid of a high-interest balance.

For example, let's say you have a credit card with a balance of $10,000 at 20 percent. If you were to transfer this balance to a card with zero percent APR for twelve months, you could save $2000 in a year ($10,000 X 20% = $2000).

It's important to understand that the low rate applies only to balance transfers. If you make any purchases on the card, you will pay a higher rate. So if the regular rate is high, use the credit card only for the balance transfers. And try to pay off the balance while you still have the introductory rate, before the regular rate takes effect.

Also remember the balance transfer fees that many companies charge. A typical fee is 3 percent of the balance transferred, up to a maximum of $75 (though some fees have no limit). Try to find a card with no balance transfer fee.

How important is it to pay your balances in full by the due date?

Credit card companies hope that their customers will not pay their full balances by the due date; that's how they make their money. But you can avoid paying any interest. Credit cards offer a grace period—the time between the statement end date and the payment due date, typically thirty days. If you pay your balance in full during the grace period, you won't be charged any interest. But once you leave a balance on a card beyond the payment due date, you start paying interest on that balance and on every additional purchase you make.

The single most effective way to maintain a low interest rate on credit cards or loans is by paying at least minimum payments by the due date. Credit companies are just waiting for you to default on one single payment so they can assess a penalty and increase your rate. Be careful with low-interest cards; read the fine print and find out what happens to your rate in the event of a late payment.

How do I avoid extra charges?

Most major credit cards offer a free on-line account, so you can check your card activity whenever you want. Some companies also offer a free e-mail reminder service to alert you when your due date is approaching. By either of these methods, you can avoid late fees, as well as over-limit fees and the like.

Before you apply for any credit, read the terms and conditions. Look for cards with no annual fees. Also read the fine print about the APR; unless it specifies that you'll keep the same rate until your balance is paid off, the company can increase your rate without notice. The term "fixed rate" can be misleading and does not guarantee that the rate will not change.

Avoid solicitations from companies offering to help you rebuild your credit through the use of "secured" credit cards marketed to "bad credit history" consumers. Many, if not all, require a secured deposit. Then they charge you an annual fee for the privilege of borrowing back your own money.

What should I do if I find an unauthorized charge on my card? What if my card is stolen?

One advantage to having on-line access to your account is that you can monitor it more frequently for unauthorized charges. If you see any questionable charges, your card—or at least your number—may have been stolen. If this happens, or if you discover a card missing, call the credit card company immediately and freeze the account until the matter is settled. You should also send a letter to the company stating the date, amount, and store where the charge occurred. You're obligated to dispute any charges that you believe are fraudulent. The company will open an investigation to assist you with the fraud review process.

Take a few preventative measures. Limit yourself to carrying only one or two cards, leaving any others locked up at home or in a safety deposit box (or in a block of ice), so you'll know almost immediately if one is missing. Record all of your credit card numbers and the customer service number that's on the back of each card, and put the information in at least two places so that you can easily access it if you need to.

What are the pros and cons of debit cards?

ATM debit cards can be great. They're convenient and you know you're paying from money you actually have; you're not incurring a debt. But if you don't diligently update your balance, you may find yourself out of cash and paying overdraft fees. Consider monitoring your balance on-line. Also keep your account balance relatively low in case of identity theft. Debit cards aren't always insured for theft.

Speaking of identity theft, how can I protect myself?

As identity thieves have become more sophisticated, insurance companies and financial institutions are offering consumers a number of tools to protect themselves. If you own a home, you might consider adding ID theft coverage as an endorsement on your existing homeowner policy. For a nominal annual premium, this insurance provides personalized counselors in the case of a theft, and it covers some legal fees and lost wages. Before talking to your insurance agent, search the web with the keywords "ID theft insurance" and read some of the articles for and against it. Also, pay a visit to the Insurance Information Institute's website at www.iii.org.

For on-line shopping, you can use a secure payment service like Paypal. This provides some protection of your personal information, but it isn't foolproof. To be totally secure, you can buy a prepaid credit card from a local grocery store, then refill it as needed. This keeps your bank account out of the purchasing picture and your information secure.

What's the best way to protect myself from fraud?

In the Internet age, many people have access to your identity. In fact, one of the most common types of fraud is called "phishing." Unsuspecting consumers receive real-looking e-mails offering loans or some other service or product, and instructing the recipient to enter bank account information, maiden name, social security number, or driver's license information. It takes only those four pieces of personal information to successfully recreate your identity! No legitimate bank will send you an e-mail requesting such sensitive information—especially your own bank, which already has it.

In their solicitations, "phishers" also typically use inflated language that's exciting or upsetting (but always false). Take a second and really look at what they're saying before you click. Think about whether the claims make sense, and note any requests for personal information. Finally, if the message claims to come from your own credit card company, call the number on the back of your card and ask the company to verify the authenticity of the message.

Here are a few more common-sense prevention tactics: Limit the use of your social security number; don't carry your social security card in your wallet or write your number on your checks. Shred important documents. Use passwords containing both letters and numbers (not your mother's maiden name). Protect all login information; don't share it or write it down near your computer.

A growing number of websites—like www.identitytheft.org, www.

privacyrights.org, www.consumer.gov/idtheft, and www.antiphishing. org—offer valuable information and tips.

Do I need credit card insurance?

Credit card insurance falls into the category of payment protection insurance and is available for loans, credit card balances, mortgages, and virtually any other long-term installment plan. They sometimes belong in your bag of financial tricks, but there may be better ways to protect yourself in case of job loss, emergency, or disaster. Always read the fine print before you enroll.

I'm in serious debt from student loans. How can I ever build a solid future, while digging out of the hole?

See if you can get a job that provides repayment assistance. For example, if you're studying to become a lawyer, a law firm may consider offering assistance as a benefit.

Another option is to put a certain percentage of your paycheck into a savings account to go toward your loan. Student loan companies also offer graduated repayment plans that gradually increase your repayment amounts on an income-sensitive basis. Call your lender and ask what assistance is available. Debt payments of more than 20 percent of your income severely limit your future financial health.

Is it safe to pay bills on-line?

This is safe for the most part, and it's useful to set up a free on-line bill payment account with your major banking institutions and utility services. Make sure they use Thawte, Verisign, or a similar security service to encrypt your data. However, this doesn't fully protect you from dishonest employees who have access to your information. But then, this is a danger in any financial institution, including the bricks-and-mortar bank down the block.

Is it safe to give out my bank account number, especially on the web?

No, this is *not* a good idea, unless you have a pre-established relationship with the requesting party, and they have secure services for information transmissions. If the relationship and the protective measures are in place, it's generally safe. Otherwise, do *not* provide any personal information.

What do you think about services that let you borrow against your next paycheck?

I'll bet you can already guess the answer to that one. If you need to borrow against money that you haven't yet been paid, you're facing a flashing red light and a screeching siren. The reason you're in this fix is that your financial situation is so bad that you've exhausted your credit or simply don't have any. You aren't managing the money that you have, and you have no reserve funds for an emergency car repair or a trip to the hospital.

If you use one of these services on a one-time basis during a really serious crisis (not just to buy that great pair of marked-down shoes), recognize that you might have a problem, and take it as a warning that you must regain control. By making a habit of paying super-high interest on your hard-earned money, you're reducing your own buying power and relinquishing real control over your money.

To avoid the problem, start a rainy day fund and feed it regularly with automatic direct deposits from your paycheck. Also put any leftover change in a container and periodically add it to your emergency fund. Give up a couple of those lattes each week and put the money in reserve. Cut down smoking or, better yet, give it up entirely and put away the money. Pack your lunch one more day each week. Give up soda a few days a week. The places to find this hidden money are virtually endless.

I'm getting a ton of "loan consolidation" solicitations in the mail. When does it make sense to use one of these, and what are the pitfalls?

Many companies offer "loan consolidation." Some of these companies are reputable, but many are not. They claim to reduce your interest rates on credit cards and other debts, and they typically promise that the consolidation will raise your FICO score. Generally you work out a monthly payment plan to pay off the debts over a few years.

However, this may *not* help your credit situation and might actually ruin your credit. Please do your research.

When should I and shouldn't I used my social security number?

You should never give your social security number out unless it's related to a banking transaction, such as a mortgage application or a car purchase. It's not required for eBay purchases or for other on-line transactions.

What are the dangers of cosigning a loan?

When you cosign on a loan, you're financially and legally responsible for the entire amount if the other signer defaults. This is never a good idea, especially if the person isn't related to you or isn't fully capable of repaying the debt.

When is bankruptcy a viable alternative?

Many people mistakenly believe that filing for bankruptcy will simply wipe the slate clean. Not so. A bankruptcy is a large black mark on your credit report for seven to ten years. However, tragedies and financial upheavals happen, and bankruptcy is a viable alternative when you've exhausted all means to resolve the solution, without success. Please seek wise counsel from an attorney or your CPA, and consider all of the alternatives.

There are four main types of bankruptcies in the United States:

- Chapter 7 bankruptcy is sometimes called a "straight bankruptcy," and is basically a liquidation proceeding. The debtor turns over all nonexempt property to the bankruptcy trustee, who then converts it to cash for distribution to the creditors. Nonexempt property varies from state to state but may include your money market funds, bonds, second home, or second car. The debtor receives a discharge from "dischargeable debts," like credit cards, back rent, or outstanding utility bills—anything that's unsecured…that has no collateral attached to it.
- Chapter 13 bankruptcy is also known as a "reorganization bankruptcy." This allows you to pay off your debts over three to five years. Please know that the law changed in October 2005, requiring at least partial payments toward debts by those who can afford it.
- Chapter 11 bankruptcy, also known as a "corporate bankruptcy," is used by businesses.
- Chapter 12 allows farmers with real estate debts to pay off the debts from the money generated by future crops.

A FINAL WORD ON HURDLING FINANCIAL STUMBLING BLOCKS

No matter where you've been financially—from simple budget problems to bankruptcy—please know that you can and will overcome these challenges. Most of us have wrestled with credit problems at least once in our lives. Even Donald Trump has faced bankruptcy, but has come back on the financial scene even stronger. With a TV show to boot!

By now you have the tools to give you a realistic view of your financial situation today and to budget for tomorrow. Next, you'll learn about how to get a team in place—people you can call for advice.

You also have access to the God of all resources. Yes, He does care about you and your money, and you haven't been left to overcome these challenges alone. Just ask for help and watch what happens! The apostle Paul writes, "My God will supply all your needs according to His riches in glory in Christ Jesus" (Philippians 4:19).

CHAPTER THREE

Getting Professional Help

Pride only breeds quarrels, but wisdom
is found in those who take advice.
PROVERBS 13:10, NIV

People have many questions and concerns about money, and that requires knowing who to ask. First you must decide how much you can (or want to) invest. Then you have to determine where and how to do it. And on it goes. You'll likely question yourself every step of the way. You'll overcome one hurdle, and another will pop up in front of you.

If you feel this way, you're not alone. At least, you shouldn't be. Taking charge of your money means taking charge of your team.

Think of your investment strategy as a relay race. You go as far as you can and then hand the baton to someone who can take over where you left off. The smart investor surrounds herself with a team of advisers who are professionals in their respective fields—stocks, mutual funds, real estate, finances, tax laws, and more. Unless you've got degrees in law, business, and accounting, *and* you're a licensed stockbroker and real estate agent, you're going to have to rely on the knowledge and skills of others in order to avoid costly errors.

But before you solicit free investment advice from your hairdresser's bookkeeper or your cousin's neighbor's insurance agent, do your homework. Their "unofficial" input might be helpful, but you need to spot the overinflated braggarts spewing dollar signs and touting their investment prowess. At the other extreme, don't be discouraged by woeful naysayers who simply didn't invest smartly. You need to join up with someone who knows where he's going, or you'll blindly follow the blind into disaster.

With investing, one size does *not* fit all. Your investment goals are different from those of your friends, neighbors, family members, and coworkers. So you need advisers who will help you develop a strategy based on *your* individual objectives. Here are some guidelines for gathering the right financial team.

THE FINANCIAL PLANNER AND THE INVESTMENT ADVISER

Before you can implement your financial strategy, you need a plan. This is your road map to success. Sure, there's something to be said for the adventure of just seeing where the road leads. But do you really want to leave your financial future up to chance?

A financial planner's job is to get you started. Whether you're looking to buy a new home, save for your child's education, plan for retirement, or just get a grip on your finances, the services of a good financial planner or free counselor can help you map out the best route. After looking at your current financial situation and discussing your goals, a financial planner will develop a plan to make your vision a reality. This could involve creating a budget, establishing a savings strategy, exploring investments, planning for taxes or retirement…or all of the above.

Do I need a financial planner?

The answer is a definite "maybe." If you have the time to research opportunities, as well as evaluate risk versus reward, you might be able to handle the task with the help of some personal finance software and books. Here are a few questions to answer before making your decision:

- Can you accurately assess your affordable level of risk?
- Do you know how to adjust your finances to respond to life changes like a birth, sudden illness, inheritance, or job loss?
- Are you confident you're handling your financial matters to your best advantage?
- Are you aware of the various opportunities available for adjusting your portfolio?
- Can you forecast how certain financial decisions can improve or detract from other areas of your plan?
- Are you up to date on changes in tax laws that could impact your situation?

If you didn't answer yes to most of these questions, consider hiring a financial planner, at least to get you started and provide direction when you need it.

What's the difference between a financial planner and a certified financial planner?

No state or federal laws exist that require a financial planner to be certified. So professionals with a broad variety of backgrounds call themselves financial planners. But the designation CFP (Certified Financial Planner) indicates both commitment and experience. To become a CFP, a financial planner has to fulfill stringent criteria established by the Certified Financial Planner Board of Standards (see them at www.cfp.net). Candidates must also accumulate three years of qualified work experience and must pass the CFP® Certification Examination, covering insurance, investment planning, tax planning, retirement planning, employee benefits, and estate planning. And effective January 1, 2007, a college degree is an additional prerequisite for the CFP.

Is a financial planner the same as an investment adviser?

Not necessarily. An investment adviser gives recommendations about specific investments, such as stocks, bonds, and mutual funds. An investment adviser might also manage portfolios and securities. A financial planner, on the other hand, develops a comprehensive strategy for a broader array of financial concerns, such as retirement and estate planning, insurance, and taxes. While most financial planners are investment advisers, don't assume that an investment adviser can deliver the type of big-picture guidance you need.

Investment advisers are not licensed, but they must register either with the Securities and Exchange Commission or with the securities agency in the state where they're doing business.

How is a financial planner or investment adviser paid?

Practices vary, so you should ask a consultant how she charges before hiring her. Payment might be a percentage of the value of the assets she manages for you. Or it might be an hourly rate or a fixed fee. With any payment arrangement, particularly fixed fees, be certain you understand what's included for the price. Ask your consultant to alert you when you ask for a service that will involve an additional fee or commission. And don't be afraid to ask for a detailed explanation of charges in advance. A planner who's genuinely concerned for your financial health will respect your need to understand the cost of doing business. If she doesn't, move on.

How can I be sure I'm getting good advice if my adviser also receives commissions from other parties?

Ask the consultant who else benefits from the advice he provides you. For example, does he receive referral rewards if you use a certain attorney? Who benefits when you purchase insurance or securities? It's also fair to ask for the approximate percentage or premium the consultant receives when you purchase financial products. Be clear about potential conflicts of interest, and ask for a written disclosure of any relationships connected to your plan and its execution.

Do I have enough assets to warrant hiring a planner?

A financial planner can help you make best use of your money, no matter how much that may be. While some advisers require you to have a minimum net worth, you'll find just as many, if not more, who'll gladly work with someone with limited assets.

What services should I expect?

The services a financial planner may offer are determined by her certifications and licenses. Selling insurance, mutual funds, or stocks requires a license. As I've already mentioned, a consultant cannot charge you for investment advice without being registered with the SEC or the state securities agency. So you first need to ask the prospective consultant what she can offer, and be sure she has the proper credentials. Ask what experience she has that is relevant to your needs (for example, planning for retirement, investment, tax issues, or estate planning).

You should also discuss the consultant's approach to financial planning. Does she prefer a cautious or aggressive strategy? Remember, any competent planner, adviser, or broker should ask you about your goals and risk tolerance. You are the final decision-maker here. Ask for examples of others she's helped reach their goals. And be sure to find out if she plans to be involved in the implementation of the plan or simply wants to develop it.

How do I check their credentials?

If the financial planner is certified, you can verify this and look for any disciplinary issues at www.cfp.net. Or call the CFP Board at 888-237-6275.

An investment adviser files a form called a Form ADV with either the SEC or the state securities agency where he's registered. The ADV provides information about the practitioner (education, experience, and any problems with regulators or clients), as well as his services, fees, and strategies. The adviser can provide you a copy of the form with his information, or, if he's registered with the state, you can contact the North American Securities Administrators Association (www.nasaa.org or call 202-737-0900). The SEC will charge a small fee. Contact the Office of Public Reference, Room 1580, 100 F Street NE, Washington, DC 20549-2521. Or visit www.sec.gov, call 202-551-8090, or email publicinfo@sec.gov.

If the adviser mentions an unfamiliar certification, ask for the governing organization, ask what the certification signifies, and ask about the requirements for earning it. Contact the governing organization to verify the consultant's standing and to determine if he has any disciplinary actions on record. Keep asking questions until you get your answers.

What else should I know about a financial planner before making my choice?

Find out how long the planner has been practicing, where, and with what types of clients. How many clients is the consultant currently managing? Be aware that in some firms you may interview and hire a specific planner only to discover you're reassigned to someone else. Ask if other individuals will handle your account. In addition to office personnel, this might include an outside accountant, an insurance agent, or a lawyer. You should meet with every individual who will have access to your information and who'll be working on your plan.

Life changes. You start a family, lose a spouse, inherit unexpected funds, buy or sell a home—all situations for which you may need help adapting. Tax laws change as well, turning yesterday's investments into today's liabilities. A good financial planner can help you understand your options and give you advice in your new circumstances.

Don't wait until you experience a crisis to establish a relationship with a financial planner. She might help you avoid such a crisis altogether.

THE ACCOUNTANT

Another key member of your financial team is your accountant. Not to be confused with a bookkeeper, the accountant analyzes financial transactions; a bookkeeper records them. An accountant reviews your financial history, identifies problems and trends, and can forecast projections. With changes in tax laws, a knowledgeable professional can steer you clear of problems and offer advice for making the best use of advantages in the tax system.

If I have a bookkeeper, why do I need an accountant?

A bookkeeper, even a "full-charge" one, should not be expected to grasp all the complexities involved in taxes, investments, and financial planning. Even the savviest full-charge bookkeeper is not qualified to handle more than the day-to-day financial management of your business. Would you want your family doctor to perform open heart surgery on you? Do you want the guy who pumps your gas to rebuild the engine on your vintage sports car? Not if you expect the best results.

Is a CPA the same as an accountant?

A Certified Public Accountant (CPA) is an accountant who has qualified for a license by completing 150 hours of college-level business courses and passing a series of extremely challenging exams. Then the CPA must complete 120 hours of continuing education hours every three years to maintain the certification, thus guaranteeing that she remains current on accounting practices.

When do I need a CPA instead of an accountant?

Businesses, as well as individuals with complex financial matters, often seek a CPA. In addition to the greater knowledge and experience, a CPA brings several other advantages. Whereas an accountant can only prepare your tax return, a CPA is authorized to *file* your return, sign financial statements, perform business audits or reviews, and represent you before the IRS, if necessary.

What is an enrolled agent?

Situated somewhere between an accountant and a CPA, an enrolled agent is often a former IRS employee—someone who understands federal and state tax laws. After passing an exam, an enrolled agent is then permitted to file your tax return and to represent you before the IRS.

How do I find an accountant?

Ask people you know about accountants they have used, and find out if they were satisfied with the service. Was the accountant responsive? Was the work neat and organized? Was work completed in a timely manner? Ask your lawyer, banker, financial planner, or investment adviser for recommendations. Find out who's working for businesses comparable in size to yours. Make a list and then get on the phone and start interviewing your prospects.

What should I ask when I interview accountants?

Ask about their credentials—their education, certifications, licenses, and experience. How long have they been practicing? What services do they provide? For CPAs, ask when and where they received their license. For those who aren't CPAs, you'll want to know how they're keeping up with changes in tax laws. And be sure to ask about the accountant's fees.

How much should I expect to pay an accountant?

The fee will depend on the complexity of your work and the services you require. If you walk into an accountant's office a week before the tax filing deadline with a shoebox overflowing with receipts, you can expect either to be hustled out the door or to pay a premium.

Be careful to avoid a tax accountant who…

- bases his fee on the amount of your return or guarantees a refund. This person has a vested interest in finding questionable shortcuts.
- isn't willing to sign his name to your return. Ask at the outset if he will sign the return. If not, move on down your list of prospects.

THE ATTORNEY

An attorney does more than get you out of legal jams. You are wise to view your attorney as a team member who can help you *avoid* legal problems. The intricate web of laws that govern taxes, estates, real estate, investments, intellectual property, and businesses are far beyond the reach of the average layperson. Your attorney can help you ethically use the legal system to your advantage. Put aside the stereotype of the ambulance-chaser with the tiny office behind the laundromat, and find yourself an experienced legal mind for your team.

Can I hire one attorney to handle all of my legal matters?

Like physicians, lawyers have specialties, such as tax, litigation, estates and trusts, family law, and real estate. If your legal issues span more than one practice area, you probably will need more than one attorney. You might establish a relationship with a law practice comprised of several lawyers with different specialties. The larger the firm, the more areas of practice they will cover.

If, however, your needs are focused primarily in one or two areas, you could probably hire just one attorney. If a problem arises that exceeds this lawyer's expertise, ask for a referral to someone with more experience in that specialty.

I've heard about boutique firms. What are they?

The term "boutique firm" refers to a small firm that focuses on and gains more experience in a specific area of law. But don't look for too many sale prices at this type of boutique!

Do I really need a lawyer if I have a qualified accountant and financial planner?

Don't confuse *having* a lawyer (accessible for service) with *using* a lawyer. Having a lawyer doesn't mean you're constantly paying for one. You should establish a relationship with one or more attorneys, depending on your legal matters, who understand your situation, your concerns, and your goals. Keep your lawyer up to date on any changes in your life or business that might impact your legal situation. If you have an impending marriage or divorce, have plans to buy or sell property, or are thinking of starting or selling a business, consult with your lawyer to uncover any avoidable problems and ensure that you're protected. An attorney can help only when kept apprised of your situation, plans, and ideas. Usually they charge on an hourly basis.

If I have a CPA, do I need a tax lawyer as well?

Not necessarily. CPAs, by their advanced training, can usually handle your tax questions. If you need legal representation, your CPA will certainly advise you, and may refer you to the right legal professional.

Do I need to put a lawyer on retainer?

If your needs are infrequent, it's not necessary to pay a monthly retainer in order to have access to your lawyer when needed. A retainer benefits only the business or individual with more complex and ongoing legal issues.

How do I find an attorney?

As with other professionals, start by asking for referrals. Once you've identified your legal needs, ask people with similar needs whom they would recommend. You can also contact the Bar Association in your state for a list of attorneys and their practice areas. Once you have a few names, call to schedule a consultation, making sure there's no cost for this initial meeting. During this consultation, you can ask about the attorney's relevant experience, discuss your needs, and inquire about fees. You have no obligation to hire the attorney on the spot, and you may want to check some references, if you haven't already done so.

THE ESTATE PLANNER

You might think you can skip over this team member, and you may be right. Then again, after you determine your net worth (as explained in the first chapter), an estate planner might suddenly become much more important to you. Once you total the value of your home, your cars, jewelry, investments, retirement accounts, life insurance policies and annuities, furnishings (especially antiques), and other property, you might be pleasantly surprised by your own net worth.

Now imagine that the worst happens, and your family has the unhappy task of disbursing your assets. If you didn't take the time to plan ahead, your estate could be taxed at a rate as high as 50 percent of the value *and* could be tied up in probate court! Instead of your loved ones receiving the fruits of your life's work, the government then takes an unhealthy share that could have been minimized with the right planning.

The federal estate tax is supposed to be repealed so do I really need to worry about the tax consequences?

The federal estate tax is expected to be repealed in 2010. But you need to protect your assets in the meantime. Besides, what if the repeal is repealed? There's still time for Congress to have a change of heart on the matter, leaving your property exposed to excessive taxation.

I have a will. Isn't that enough?

A will allows for the distribution of your property after your death and is essential to avoid the lengthy delays if your estate has to go through probate. But an estate plan addresses other important issues. For example, you can create a trust for your spouse or children, ensuring their financial security. You can establish a power of attorney in the event that you become incapacitated and unable to handle your financial matters. If, for example, you suffer a debilitating stroke and need to be cared for in a nursing home or other residential facility, your spouse may not be able to access the funds to pay for the nursing home, let alone maintain your home. An estate plan can also outline your wishes for a funeral and burial.

How do I find an estate planner?

The National Association of Estate Planners and Councils (www.naepc. org) is a national organization that awards the certification of Accredited Estate Planner (AEP), and can help you find an individual with the knowledge and experience you need.

THE STOCKBROKER

A stockbroker—also called a "registered representative"—is paid to buy and sell securities on your behalf through the stock exchange. The veil of secrecy around the once-elite corps of financial visionaries has been thrown aside with the onset of discount brokerage houses and on-line trading. Now the trading game is more affordable to the average investor.

A broker must earn certification by passing the General Securities Registered Representative Exam administered by the National Association of Securities Dealers (NASD). She must also complete four months of on-the-job training to understand trading procedures. Some states also require a broker to pass the Uniform Securities Agents State Law Examination.

How much do I need to invest to get started?

Ask the broker if he requires a minimum deposit. If you're not comfortable with the amount, find another broker. These minimums vary, and some brokerage firms have none. So don't feel pressured to invest more than you can.

Can a stockbroker also provide me with financial planning help?

If the broker is also a registered investment adviser or certified financial planner, you can get additional assistance. However, the primary job of the broker is to handle your stock trades, not manage your financial planning.

How is the broker paid?

First of all, you pay the broker a commission on the trades (purchases and sales) she makes for you. She may also charge fees for transferring assets, closing an account, wire transfers, inactive accounts, not maintaining a minimum balance, and IRA custodian fees. Ask your broker about her fee schedule before you start racking up excess—and avoidable—charges.

How do I choose a broker?

As with the other professionals you hire, ask family, friends, and colleagues for recommendations. Ask your potential broker if he offers particular mutual funds that pique your interest. Discuss trading philosophy, the types of clients the broker works with, and what types of returns you can reasonably expect. And check the broker's credentials with the NASD Central Registration Depository (800-289-9999).

What service can I expect?

Money does talk with stockbrokers; more money speaks more loudly. But regardless of the amount you're investing, you should expect prompt responses to your requests. During your initial interview, ask who will be responsible for your account and whom to contact with questions. Find out about on-line access to your account. Check the brokerage firm's website to see if it's easy to navigate; don't spend your precious time clicking and waiting. Trading is all about timing, and brokers are used to a fast pace, so it's reasonable to expect the website to be speedy as well.

THE REAL ESTATE AGENT

A home is the single biggest investment most people will make in their lifetime. Whether you're buying property as a primary residence or strictly for investment purposes, you'll most likely deal with a real estate professional. This individual can help you find the right property, analyze market value, identify potential structural or resale concerns, make the deal, and even direct you to financing opportunities. A real estate professional achieves success by building a network of positive relationships. Even if one home is all you ever purchase, you're an important client, because you are a source of crucial word-of-mouth advertising. (More on taking charge of your real estate in chapter 7.)

Is there any difference between a real estate agent, a broker, and a realtor?

A real estate agent is a salesperson. In most states, agents are required to be licensed, which means they have to study and pass an examination covering all aspects of real estate transactions, including financing and legal concerns. A broker is usually an agent with more extensive education and experience. A broker can run his or her own real estate business; an agent cannot. All monies and escrow accounts are managed under one broker's license for each office.

The term "Realtor®" designates an agent or broker who's a member of the National Association of Realtors®, an organization of more than 700,000 real estate professionals subscribing to a strict code of ethics.

What is a buyer's agent?

A buyer's agent works on the buyer's behalf, guarding the buyer's interests. The selling agent, by contrast, tries to sell property at the highest possible price, through marketing techniques such as advertising and hosting an open house. When the house is sold, the commission is split between the selling agent and the buyer's agent. In some cases, these might be the same person, which is why an agent will try to promote her own listing to prospective customers.

Why should I pay a commission to an agent when I can sell my house myself?

An experienced real estate agent or broker knows how to identify good and bad deals in the market. Real estate agents know property values and how to properly show a home to a prospective buyer. They have experience with the paperwork and legal issues associated with the transaction, and have likely encountered and sailed over many hurdles that could trip you up if you're on your own. For a seller, a licensed agent can give you advice for making your home more appealing to buyers. Plus, a professional can protect you from buyer's agents who try to take advantage of your inexperience. A recent NAR survey[2] showed that the median price for a home sold with the assistance of a real estate professional was 13 percent higher than for those sold by owner. With the approximately 6-percent commission paid to an agent or broker, you would still end up with a higher profit by relying on professional help.

How do I find the right agent for me?

Of course, you should always ask around for recommendations, but here are a few other ideas. Look in the real estate section of your local paper, or in one of the many real estate magazines available in your local grocery store.

Check for homes comparable to yours in terms of location and price range and see who the agent is, in order to find someone with experience marketing a home like yours. Attend an open house to see the agent in action. Is he personable and knowledgeable or too pushy? Has he made an effort to learn about the house he's selling? Make a consultation appointment with this agent; good agents won't charge you for this initial meeting.

What questions should I ask a prospective agent?

Once you've narrowed your list, talk to each agent about her approach to representing your needs (whether buying or selling). Ask how she handles issues like alternative financing and fielding low-ball offers. If you're seeking to buy a home in a different area, see if the agent is knowledgeable about issues like local taxes, the quality of the school system, neighborhoods, and area businesses. Ask how long she has held a license, if she's a member of NAR, and how many home sales she's closed in the past six months. Discuss with the agent how she'll market your home, and ask her to demonstrate any high-tech advertising strategies she uses.

If you're hiring a listing agent, ask for the ratio of sold-to-asking price for her listings. This is particularly important when an agent tries to "buy" your listing by promising to sell your home for a higher price. The large dollar signs might woo you, but in the end you might have to settle for a lower price than you would have if you'd priced it reasonably to begin with. The longer a house stays on the market, the less desirable it is. You lose the initial flurry of interested buyers who bite at new listings, and you become prey to agents who think you're desperate to sell.

REVIEWING YOUR TEAM ROSTER

We're living in a do-it-yourself society, enhanced by all the free information available through the Internet. Certain software programs can empower you to do your own taxes, write your own will, and accomplish a few other tasks. But none of these resources provide the experience, knowledge, and insight a trained professional can offer to help you make the final decisions about your money. While you might not need to hire every service provider listed in this chapter, you should at least understand who's available if and when you need them. Remember, you're assembling a team to support your goal of financial success. If some players have to sit on the bench until you need them, at least they're close by and know the plays when you call them into action.

Finally and foremost, before you begin, don't forget to ask advice of the best financial adviser of all, the God of all resources. If you put your needs and concerns before Him, He'll help you find the right strategy and team. "If any of you lacks wisdom, let him ask of God, who gives to all generously and without reproach, and it will be given to him" (James 1:5).

PART II

Consider Your Field
of Investment

CHAPTER FOUR

The Market (No, Not the Supermarket) Made Easy

But the master replied, "You wicked and lazy servant! You think I'm a hard man, do you, harvesting crops I didn't plant and gathering crops I didn't cultivate? Well, you should at least have put my money into the bank so I could have some interest."

MATTHEW 25:26–27, NLT

In the Bible's Parable of the Talents, a man entrusted his employees with money to invest. But when the boss learned that one lazy guy had buried his money in the ground "for safekeeping," the boss rebuked him harshly. "You could at least have earned a little interest." This man was punished, while the employees who doubled their boss's money were rewarded.

In today's market, earning interest on our money is the very least we can do to be good stewards of our finances. The days have long passed when your only option was a savings account; now you have a wide range of choices to put your dollars to work for you. Sticking your funds in a checking account, where you gain nothing but access, will not take you even one baby step toward financial security. While you're sitting on your money, the cost of living is rising; you're not even keeping up with inflation. You're falling behind when you could surge ahead. So where do you begin?

You've heard your friends, families, and coworkers boast about their portfolios, talk about market fluctuations, and discuss their windfall from smart investing. You've steered clear of this whole enterprise because the world of high finance seemed too complex, but now you're ready to get involved and start making some money. What's involved in stocks, commodities, mutual funds, and more retirement fund options than you can count?

That question is the reason for this chapter. Together we'll gently wade through the raging waters of investment and the various opinions that lie therein. Don't dive in head first, or you'll be swept away. Dip in one toe and gradually get the feel of it. By the end of this chapter you'll be conversant in StockSpeak, able to identify your investment needs. You'll be familiar with at least some of the options available to you and how to evaluate those choices to make your own decisions.

So let's go test the water....

INVESTMENT CHOICES

You've decided that investing is a smart way to improve your financial outlook. Now you're presented with a range of choices, from cautious to high-risk—options that tempt you with the prospect of hefty returns. Where do you start? Should you take some risks, or do you have the temperament to dive into the deep end of the investment pool?

Terms

Bonds are like an IOU. When you purchase a bond, you agree to lend money to a company or government for a specific time period at a predetermined interest rate. A company issues a bond in lieu of offering stock in order to boost cash flow without selling off ownership and giving up partial control.

A *CD*, or certificate of deposit, represents a short-term investment, between three months and five years, maybe more. When you purchase a CD, you're lending money to the bank for a defined period at a guaranteed rate of return (interest rate). CDs are insured by the FDIC and provide a nominal return at virtually no risk. There are penalties (fees) for withdrawing money from your CD before the term has ended.

Commodities are natural products, like beef, wheat, coffee, cocoa, gold, and oil. This market is referred to as "futures," since it's based on speculation surrounding the upcoming production of the materials. As a result, commodities have a limited "shelf life," in contrast to the purchase of a long-term stock.

IRA stands for "Individual Retirement Account," a retirement plan option created by the Internal Revenue Service (IRS). You make voluntary contributions to the account and gain certain tax advantages, depending on the type of IRA you choose. Inside the IRA, you have the ability to invest in CDs, money market accounts, bonds, stocks, and mutual funds.

A *money market account* is a savings account at a financial institution. The bank invests the money in short-term securities, such as CDs or U.S. Treasury bills (T bills). A money market account usually pays a higher return than a traditional savings account.

Mutual funds are investment vehicles in which companies (like Janus and Fidelity) pool money from shareholders and invest that money in various investments—stocks, bonds, options, commodities, or money market accounts. Each mutual fund is guided by a particular investment objective stated in its charter. A mutual fund may be very conservative or very aggressive depending upon its investment objective.

A *portfolio* is your collected investments, which might include stocks, bonds, money markets, and other securities. The word "securities" refers to the paper certificates or electronic records showing your ownership.

Stock is partial ownership in a company. When a business needs to raise capital, it divides itself into small pieces—shares of stock—and sells them to people who want to invest with hopes of making a profit on the company's success. In exchange for these possible higher returns, the buyer assumes a risk that some or all of the investment may be lost. When you purchase shares of stock, you become a stockholder or shareholder. Unlike a bond, a stock is not a loan that will be repaid.

What are my options?

A CD or money market account represent no-risk methods for making your money start working for you. The returns are small in comparison to other options, but any of these choices is better than doing nothing at all.

The next option to consider is a bond. You'll likely be committing your cash to a longer period of investment, but you should also expect a higher return for your patience. Know that it's possible for a bond to fluctuate in value between the time of purchase and its maturity.

Mutual funds, stocks, and commodities take you into a more competitive arena. The choices are seemingly limitless once you begin to explore the products that are available. And they are products; you are the consumer making a purchase. Many investment advisers consider commodities to be risky because it's possible to take a huge hit in a single day. On the other hand, mutual funds are packaged in a full range of risk levels, so if you feel uncomfortable with that market, investigate less aggressively managed funds.

How do I choose?

Before you invest your money anywhere, stop to consider your investment goals—both short- and long-term. Determine how much you can afford to invest. Don't stretch yourself too thin. A product that limits your access could pose a problem if you need quick cash. As you begin investing, think about what you'll do with any profits that you realize. Are you planning to reinvest the dividends? Do you hope to grow your portfolio? Will you use that capital to finance a business or invest in real estate?

Once you know what you need from your investment, you can narrow down the list of likely candidates. For short-term investments, a CD or money market account is probably the way to go. With a money market account, your funds are readily accessible without penalty. Early withdrawal from a CD usually involves a penalty.

To meet longer-term goals, like saving for a child's college education or for retirement, consider the various IRA options. A 529 plan offers either a prepaid tuition or savings plan where your contributions aren't taxed until withdrawn. If your investment goal is a comfortable retirement, you have many options, from a traditional IRA to a SEP, SIMPLE, or ROTH, to name just a few. More details later.

You might choose mutual funds and stocks when you're ready to invest on a larger scale. The key to "playing the market" is sticking with it. The volatility of the stock market isn't for the weak of heart. The investors who do well here are those who remain steadfastly committed for a long period, riding out the rough times for at least three to five years, preferably longer.

Depending upon how much you have to invest, you should consider using multiple investment options.

Do I need a broker?

The answer is a definite maybe. The rapid growth of on-line trading has supplanted the need for a broker intermediary. As I've already shared, my experiences with brokers taught me the art of losing money—especially through commissions, fees, and margin calls. However, not all brokers are the same. Just because you can do your own trading doesn't mean that you should. A qualified broker has made a career of studying the stock market. He or she knows the history of certain stocks, understands how to read changes in the market, and can predict trends.

A seasoned broker also has broader experience working with different investment styles and goals. You're approaching investments from your individual perspective, but a broker can explain how different people have managed their investments, both the cautious and the risk-takers. His experience gives you a broader perspective before parting with your hard-earned cash.

There is, of course, a price to pay for this wisdom. Brokers involve trading fees and other charges. You're paying for a service. The broker is in business to make money…hopefully, by providing you with profitable investment advice.

Before you decide whether or not to hire a broker to manage your portfolio, ask lots of questions. Don't be afraid to ask dumb questions, and be willing to say no just as often as you say yes. Discuss your investment goals and ask about her strategy. Does she have experience working with other investors in situations similar to your own?

Ask about fees. How can you monitor your investments? Why does he consider himself a successful investor? You should also know in advance which products he offers. Not all brokerage firms can get you into the mutual funds you want, for example. Ask for a list of the funds he represents.

When considering hiring a broker (or any investment adviser, for that matter), watch for potential bias or conflicts that could color her recommendations. Some brokers will attempt to steer you into their own products (proprietary mutual funds or annuities), so it's important that you understand your broker's own incentives.

For the newcomer to the world of stocks and mutual funds, watch your broker and learn. Consider the fees the cost of your education.

What can I expect from a discount broker?

There's always a cost associated with getting a discount. Discount brokers are no exception. These firms are designed for the do-it-yourselfer who knows what she wants to buy and sell and merely needs a vehicle for making the trades. Discount brokers don't offer financial advice, and their fees are about one-half to one-third of those for a traditional broker. Discount brokers include Ameritrade, TD Waterhouse, and E*Trade, which charge an average of eight to thirty dollars per transaction and offer user-friendly websites.

If, however, you need help or advice, don't expect it from the discount broker. Fortunately, brokerage houses like Charles Schwab, Fidelity, and Merrill Lynch offer the option of choosing between the full-service and the discounted version under the same roof.

How do I open a brokerage account?

Before you can buy stocks, bonds, mutual funds, or other securities, you need to open a brokerage account. Some firms require a minimum investment—typically $500 to $1,000—to get started.

Decide whether you want to work with a discount brokerage or a full-service brokerage firm. More than seventy on-line brokers offer varying degrees of services and fees. You can expect to pay anywhere from five to fifty dollars for a single trade, and some climb even higher. With the growing competition between brokers trawling for your business, some offer no-fee trades. As with any other tempting offer, be sure to read the fine print to learn the true cost of getting "something for nothing."

To open an account, you can usually either download an application or have one mailed to you. Fill it out and mail it in with a check. Or visit your broker's office to fill out a form and actually speak to a human being. That's my choice.

What fees will I have to pay?

The rapidly increasing number of discount brokers touting low fees has heated up the competition. Brokers need to make a living, too. So guess what? You now have additional charges on your statement. Here's a list of what you might be paying your broker:

Commission: Your broker might charge you a flat fee or a percentage of the purchase or sale—or both. Remember that when you instruct your broker to buy one stock and sell another at the same time, it still counts as two transactions and incurs two fees.

Transfer fee: A charge for transferring your stocks to another broker, to discourage you from bouncing from one broker to another. If you want to transfer an account, ask the new brokerage firm if they're willing to reimburse this fee.

Inactivity fee: When your account lies dormant for longer than your brokerage firm deems appropriate.

Account maintenance fee: For extra services like research, maintaining records, printing reports, and mailing statements. An investment adviser tells me this has become more commonplace as the baby boomer generation gets older. Also, many times this fee is associated with IRAs, due to tax reporting issues.

Minimum equity requirement fee: A penalty you incur when your account falls below the minimum balance.

Charges that might seem small at the outset could take their toll over time. For example, if you're charged twenty dollars each quarter for not maintaining the account minimum, you pay eighty dollars a year. If you purchased a $1000 bond earning 8 percent interest, your annual dividend was just absorbed by this avoidable penalty. Ask for a fee schedule and read it carefully.

Is on-line trading the way to go?

If you're a self-directed individual who needs little or no guidance, on-line trading can be a good choice. You can monitor your account and issue trade orders to your broker any time and anywhere you have access to the Internet. Ask your broker about on-line services available to you.

PLAYING THE STOCK MARKET

The stock market can appear to be a perplexing maze, a crap shoot, or a thrill ride. Those movies that portray flailing, shouting traders on the stock exchange floor further enhance the perception of insanity. Indeed, fortunes can be made and lost in the midst of this fast-paced adventure.

So let's reduce the stock market to simpler terms. When you buy stock in a company, you're purchasing a piece of it. The company that offers stock is seeking to raise capital. They want money coming in without the pressure of repaying a debt, like a loan or bond. In return, the owners give up partial ownership. They still maintain a controlling interest (51 percent or more), but now have certain responsibilities to all the other shareholders, like turning a profit or explaining why they're not.

While there are intricacies involved in investing in the stock market, the basic idea is that you purchase stock and earn a per-share dividend when the company makes a profit. If, for example, you buy a stock for $10 a share and the value increases to $11.50, you've turned a 15 percent profit. On the other hand, if the stock price falls, you lose money. The trick is to understand when to buy and when to sell, and we'll cover that a little later in this chapter. In the meantime, let's explore the fundamentals of stock market investing.

Terms

Blue chip stock refers to a stock issued by a company that's a proven success and usually (emphasis on *usually*) delivers dividends to shareholders. Companies like Coca-Cola and Wal-Mart are examples.

A *bubble* describes a condition in the stock market where prices rise rapidly (and without a logical reason) above their fundamental value. With no sound basis for the growth, this bubble will eventually burst and the price will sink. (Remember the dot.com stock era?)

Bull and bear markets refer to long-term market fluctuations. A bear market is defined by a drop of at least 15 percent in each of the three major stock averages—Dow Jones Industrial, S&P 500, and Value Line Index—and can last months or years. A bull market is characterized by an upswing in the market over a period of months or years.

Common stock is the most…well…*common* type of stock issued. An investor with common stock gets one vote per share and receives higher returns, although the dividends are based on a variable rate and therefore involve greater risk.

The *Consumer Price Index* (CPI) measures the average price change for consumer goods and services, such as energy, food and beverages, housing, apparel, transportation, medical care, and entertainment. Also known as the "cost of living index," this number is calculated monthly by the U.S. Bureau of Labor Statistics. The number compares the average price paid by a typical consumer for a "basket" of goods in these categories from month to month. This isn't precise, but the CPI is the best way to keep track of inflation's toll on our everyday lifestyle.

A *dividend* is a stockholder's share of a company's profits, which are divided equally by the number of shares issued. Not all companies pay dividends—they aren't required to do so—but those that do generally issue dividend payments on a quarterly basis.

The *Dow Jones Industrial Average* is an index made up of thirty of the largest and most influential companies in the country. Established in the late 1800s by Charles Dow, this index is internationally recognized as a strong indicator of how the stock market is performing. The companies in this index span most major areas of the U.S. economy and are selected by the editors of *The Wall Street Journal*.

A *growth fund* is a stock that may not pay a regular dividend but offers potentially large capital gains.

An *income fund* is a stock that pays a regular dividend to shareholders.

An *index fund* is a portfolio of investments that reflects the performance of a stock exchange index, like Dow Jones or S&P 500.

Market capitalization is a measure of a public company's size—the total value of all outstanding shares of stock in a company, calculated by multiplying the total number of shares by the market price.

NASDAQ stands for National Association of Securities Dealers Automated Quotations System. Most technology stocks are traded through this electronic exchange.

Penny stock trades for five dollars or less per share, which makes it a risky investment, because if the stock price drops below one dollar, it will lose its listing on the stock exchange. At this point the company is either in a shaky financial situation or not far from filing for bankruptcy. Most financial advisers would advise against this risk.

Preferred stock doesn't usually provide voting rights, but does guarantee a fixed dividend, unlike the variable rate associated with common stock. In the event a company folds, preferred shareholders are paid before the common stockholders.

The *Producer Price Index* (PPI) tracks changes in wholesale prices of commodities—such as food, metals, lumber, oil, and gas—but not services. Similar to the CPI, the PPI is calculated by the U.S. Bureau of Labor Statistics and reports inflation from the manufacturer's side, which can lead to consumer cost increases. For example, when Hurricane Katrina devastated the Gulf states, more building materials were sent there to rebuild the cities. As a result, supply was strained and the cost of lumber increased in response to heavy demand.

The *S&P 500* (Standard and Poor) is a stock price index comprised of five hundred blue chip stocks that are used to measure stock market conditions. Industrial, transportation, utility, and financial companies are represented here, and many analysts believe the S&P 500 provides a more accurate measure than the Dow.

Sector funds are stocks that concentrate in a specific industry area, such as health care or technology.

Small cap stock refers to a stock with small market capitalization. "Small" in the financial world means between $250 million and $2 billion. I'll give you the lowdown on this a little later in this chapter. By the way, one notch below the small cap is the *micro cap* with less the $250 million in market capitalization. Anything below $50 million is called a *nano cap*.

A *stock split* occurs when a company increases the number of shares, perhaps to increase liquidity. Say you have one hundred shares of stock in a company at twenty dollars per share. They do a 2-1 stock split, so you now have two hundred shares worth ten dollars each. The total dollar value of your holding is the same. So why bother? The lower per-share price becomes more appealing, stimulating more buying, which improves liquidity. With more activity, the price of the stock goes up, leading to greater gains. However, with more shares on the market, the move can also backfire and create losses.

Stock yield is the dividend as a percentage of the stock price. If, for example, a stock that sells for $50 per share delivers an annual dividend of $2.50, the yield is 5 percent ($2.50/$50.00).

A *ticker symbol* is the abbreviation for a stock—like "MSFT" for Microsoft and "HD" for Home Depot—that's used as shorthand in stock listings and other communications. The number of letters in the ticker symbol indicates which exchange trades the stock. For example, NASDAQ stocks have four or more letters, like CSCO (Cisco) and DELL (Dell Computers). If a stock symbol consists of three letters or less, it trades on the New York Stock Exchange.

Value Line is an investment research service that reviews and ranks hundreds of stocks and mutual funds in terms of safety or risk, timeliness, and projected performance.

Why would I choose the stock market as my field of investment?

People get involved in the stock market for any of the following reasons:

- to increase cash flow
- as protection from taxes (as with retirement funds, for example)
- to create financial security with long-term growth

Although the stock market experiences ups and downs—sometimes drastic—stocks can still deliver a higher return over a long period of time. They're one of the few investments that grow faster than the rate of inflation. By staying ahead of the ever-increasing cost of living, you're creating a financial cushion for your eventual retirement. If you do it correctly, "eventual" can come sooner than planned, and you can spend more years enjoying the sweet rewards of your savvy investment strategy.

However, you might be concerned about the risk involved in playing the stock market. You hear about a downturn in the market. You know people who were devastated by the Black Monday market crash of 1987, and you tell yourself that you can't afford to take that chance. Here, timing is everything. If you're nearing retirement or need fast access to funds just to live on, be careful.

On the other hand, if you can invest for the long term, you may win the market game. In spite of the bottom dropping out of the market on October 19, 1987—when stocks plummeted a record 22.6 percent—people who invested wisely and remained patient came back from the crushing blow. Professor Matthew Spiegel of the Yale School of Management reported that an investor in the stock market prior to the 1987 crash who held onto his stocks would have realized an 8.8 percent compounded return by 2002.[3] Compare that to a 5.0 percent return on bonds. The key for salvaging profits from the jaws of a desperate situation was patience.

How much do I need to start?

You don't need thousands of dollars to begin your stock market venture. You'll need a brokerage account, and your broker may require a minimum investment. It's not unreasonable to open an account with as little as $500. You might start with a couple of the less expensive small-cap stocks. Pay close attention to fees, because every extra charge at this level cuts into your ability to make a profit. If you're paying thirty dollars for each transaction, your $500 isn't going to get you many shares of even a small-cap stock. Another possibility is to begin by investing in a stock mutual fund, small cap, or large cap.

Invested wisely, even a small initial cash outlay could turn a profit in a relatively short period of time. However, I repeat, the stock market isn't a place for short-term investors. The "real money" comes when you stick with it. Reinvest your profits into more stock purchases and watch your portfolio grow.

When should I start investing?

As soon as possible. The stock market delivers the best returns over the long haul so the sooner you get started, the sooner you can start growing your portfolio. Once you have the minimum amount required, get thee to a broker, discount or otherwise. I often tell younger investors to begin their investing education with the stock market, because it teaches you to manage greed and fear—two forces that drive the market. Greed when things are going well and fear when you start to see your stocks take a turn. This will help you manage your emotions, as well as managing your money.

How do I get started?

Before you start making stock market picks, do your homework. Determine your market objective. Consider this field long and hard. What do you want to accomplish? And be more specific than "make money." What's your financial goal? What's your time frame? Do you need to make a certain amount of money in a couple of years because your ten-year-old is looking like an Ivy Leaguer? Are you trying to feather your nest egg for retirement and want more than a retirement account can offer? The more specific you can be about your goals and expectations, the easier it will be to make the kind of stock decisions that will deliver the results you need.

Second, research stocks from various companies. Look at their trading history, readily available through a broker or from on-line databases. If you're an information junkie, get a copy of the company's annual report and pore over the data. Don't know where to start? Look at stocks from companies that are familiar to you. Consider businesses in your area that you can more closely monitor. I love the Charles Schwab brokerage because, not only does this company offer great research and information on-line, but it also hosts educational seminars for clients.

What is index investing?

An index is a list of stocks that measures the changes of that particular portfolio. These statistics reflect the overall market's performance—similar to a pollster's work surveying a representative sample of a population to identify characteristics, note trends, and project likely changes.

An index fund is a mutual or exchange-traded fund (ETF) that includes stocks from within a specific index, in the same proportions as the index. In effect, an index fund offers the equivalent of a low-cost mutual fund. An index fund isn't actively managed, as a mutual fund is. The fund doesn't require a stock analyst, because by definition the selection of stocks is predetermined by the index. With passive management, there are fewer transactions, which prevents costly capital gains taxes that result from selling stocks at a profit.

Index funds offer tremendous diversification. With more stocks comprising the overall index fund, you're less likely to take a hit when a few securities slide.

John C. Bogle launched the first index fund on December 31, 1975, and was ridiculed for establishing a fund that relied on index averages rather than active participation in stock watching. The fund tracked stocks from the S&P 500 and began with assets of $11 million. Later named the Vanguard 500 Index Fund, it delivered an unheard-of 50 percent annual growth rate. In 1999, the fund topped the $100 billion mark.

Different indexes represent different stocks, so you need to understand who's listing the stocks that interest you. We briefly defined the most common indexes in the first section of this chapter. Now let's take a closer look at these all-important indicators.

Dow Jones Industrial Average. In the late 1800s, the DJIA was calculated by taking the stock price of each of just twelve companies and then dividing by twelve. Today, the Dow has grown to thirty blue chip companies—the largest and most influential—as determined by the editors of *The Wall Street Journal.* The DJIA long ago replaced its "average" methodology with a more complex system for determining the DJIA, called price-based weighting. Stocks are included in proportions based on their quoted prices with the greater "weight" going to the higher priced stocks.

Plus: The Dow is the oldest and most revered of all indexes. Its stocks represent the top tier of U.S. companies, which translates to the lowest levels of risk and volatility.

Minus: Price-based weighting is considered flawed because of other factors than can affect this figure, such as stock splits. In addition, the thirty companies listed in this index represent a miniscule fraction of the more than 10,000 publicly traded companies, so the DJIA isn't an accurate snapshot of the total stock market.

S&P 500 Index. This index was created by Standard and Poor, a financial advisory, securities rating, and publishing firm. The S&P 500 Index is comprised of five hundred most widely held stocks, which aren't necessarily the largest companies. The S&P 500 represents a broad range of areas, including four hundred industrial, twenty transportation, forty utility, and forty financial companies. The weighting system is based on each company's market capitalization, so each stock is evaluated proportionately, in contrast to the DJIA method. Due largely to fallouts and mergers, anywhere from twenty-five to fifty stocks are added to and removed from the list each year. Google recently joined the S&P 500—the largest company ever to be added and the list's highest-priced member.

Plus: With five hundred companies and the market capitalization weighting system, the S&P 500 is considered a more accurate barometer of the stock market than the Dow. The diversity of stocks represents about 70 percent of the American market.

Minus: Of the five hundred companies in this index, forty-five of them account for about half of the total value, meaning less than 10 percent of the list dominates the portfolio.

NASDAQ Composite Index. This is a relatively new index that was launched in 1971 and currently includes 3,000 stocks—all of the companies that are traded on the NASDAQ. Its focus is heavily weighted toward technology and Internet companies, which spawned its quick rise in popularity as one of the premier indexes in the world. The list also includes financial, consumer, biotech, and industrial companies. A separate index—the NASDAQ 100—is comprised of the one hundred largest non-financial companies trading on NASDAQ. Like the S&P 500, the NASDAQ Composite Index is weighted by market capitalization.

Plus: The majority of stocks on this index are rooted in technology and the Internet, both high-growth areas.

Minus: These types of stocks represent higher risk and greater volatility. When technology takes a hit, so does the NASDAQ Composite Index.

Wilshire 5000 Total Market Index. This is a non-discriminating index, representing all companies traded on the New York Stock Exchange, as well as many from NASDAQ and the American Stock Exchange (Amex). Started in 1980, the index now features more than 6,500 stocks that trade in the United States, rated by the same market capitalization weighting system as many of the other indexes.

Plus: The diversity of the index reflects perhaps the most comprehensive view of the American stock market.

Minus: Like the S&P 500, a small minority of companies heavily tips the scales. In this case, 10 percent of the stocks account for 75 percent of the total value. And the index features only those companies that are headquartered in the U.S., excluding strong foreign businesses that actively trade in this country.

Russell 2000 and Russell 3000 Indexes. The Russell 3000 Index lists 3,000 of the largest U.S. companies—similar to the Wilshire index—and represents about 98 percent of the U.S. equity market. The Russell 2000 (also known as R2K) is comprised of the lower-end companies—in terms of capitalization—in the Russell 3000. Although the list accounts for two-thirds of the bigger list, these 2,000 businesses represent only about 8 percent of the total market capitalization of the bigger index. Stocks valued at one dollar or less are excluded.

Plus: The index offers tremendous diversity and a focus on small companies with growth potential.

Minus: Because of the nature of the small companies in the index, you'll see some stock spasms, with winning and losing streaks.

What causes a stock to go up or down?

Stock prices are at the mercy of supply and demand, which is often directed by flawed human behavior. When investors start selling off large numbers of stock in a certain company, the market becomes flooded with too many shares and not enough buyers. The price of the stock then drops, leaving the remaining shareholders at a loss, literally. In some cases, the reasons for selling the stock may have nothing to do with the stock's performance.

So what causes a wise shareholder to sell? Maybe the stock isn't performing up to expectations. Profits have leveled off or are declining. Or perhaps that industry as a whole has experienced some problems. Imagine the impact on pharmaceutical stocks when one FDA-approved drug comes under question. Or maybe your stock is declining because of a downturn in the overall market.

Of course, the opposite is just as likely. A stock price can increase when demand is greater than the supply. For instance, when a company expands or launches a successful product—like Microsoft, Wal-Mart, and Cisco during their boom phases—the desire to purchase stock in these winners escalates, and the stock price rises. Who doesn't want to team up with a rising star? The dream of every stock trader is to find that giant-of-tomorrow before the world notices.

How do I evaluate a stock?

There are several factors to consider. What does the company actually do? Is it in a hot growth industry or heading toward saturation? What are the annual sales? Do they appear to be leveling off and, if so, do you know why? Can you spot a trend in the company's competition?

Look at the overall value of the company. Again, the price for acquiring the company is known as *market capitalization*—the price of all outstanding shares of common stock multiplied by the quoted price per share. If you're looking at a corporation with one million shares of common stock at a price of thirty dollars per share, the company would have a market cap of $30 million. Compare this number to the company's performance. Does its revenue substantiate the investment, or does it appear inflated?

Take a look at the price-to-earnings ratio (p/e ratio)—calculated by dividing the stock price by the stock's profit in the past twelve months. If you're looking at a stock that's selling for $60 a share and has earned $2.40 over the past year, the p/e ratio is 25.0 ($60/$2.40). In contrast, a stock selling for $36 that made half as much ($1.20) has a p/e of 30.0, which is less favorable. This gives you an apples-to-apples method of comparison.

Another indicator to consider is the company's per-share growth. A company can boost the profit per share by buying back shares, reducing the number of available shares. The company's value remains the same, but shareholders are getting a bigger slice of the pie, translating into more ownership and greater profits without spending another cent! It does, however, take a visionary management team to undertake such a gutsy stock move.

You also need to examine your personal interest in a stock. Just because you love the taste of a certain brand of ice cream or believe in the environmental benefits of recycled paper products doesn't mean you should invest in a company. Don't let your emotions cloud your financial judgment.

What does it mean to diversify?

Remember the cautionary maxim, "Don't put all your eggs in one basket"? This is the philosophy behind diversification—expanding your portfolio in different directions. Concentrating all your investments within a narrow scope could prove hazardous to your financial health if that segment bottoms out. You might think you're diversified if, for example, you've bought stocks in twenty different companies. But if those companies are all concentrated in one area—like the dotcom rage of the '90s—you could have a basketful of broken eggs if that industry tanks.

You don't need to spread yourself too thin to diversify. Look at the breadth of your portfolio, including CDs, money markets, bonds, and mutual funds, to determine your vulnerability. Identify areas where you might be too heavily concentrated. If you're concerned, talk to a financial adviser—someone other than a broker—who can offer an objective perspective.

What's the difference between a primary and secondary market?

These terms refer to the markets where and when stocks are traded. When you purchase stocks from a *primary market*, you acquire them directly from the company that issues the shares. A privately held company that "goes public" offers stocks for the first time through an *initial public offering* (IPO).

A *secondary market* involves trading securities that are already out there through an initial private or pubic offering. These are the trades we've been talking about a great deal in this chapter. (Also, if you want to impress your friends at your child's next birthday party, tell them that just after a new security is issued, it's often referred to as the aftermarket. That should spur party conversation—or blank stares.) Most trades are handled by brokers buying and selling securities that have already been issued, without involving the companies that issued them. Without such systems in place, you'd spend valuable time trying to locate someone with shares in the company who's willing to make a deal with you.

What's a DRIP?

It stands for Dividend Reinvestment Program, and it's a good way to start investing in the stock market with limited funds. When you enroll in a DRIP, you buy shares at a discounted price. Then instead of coming to you by check at payout time, the dividend is automatically reinvested in shares or fractional shares. Your investment grows and you pay no commission. In "Build Your Wealth Drip by Drip,"[4] authors Jerry Edgerton and Jim Frederick estimate that if you invested $10,000 in the S&P 500 Index at the end of 1985 and didn't reinvest the dividends, you would have $29,150 by the end of 1995. Had you put those dividends back into the stocks, your total in the same time period would have exceeded $40,000.

Another investment adviser tells me that a disadvantage to a DRIP program is that you have no control over the price you buy or sell the stock for. It may take days for an execution to occur and this could result in quite a different price from the one you originally hoped for, especially with a volatile stock. The advantage is that there usually isn't a commission involved.

Should I buy and sell stock based on price alone?

The smart money says no. Before you gobble up a stock because it appears to be a bargain, determine whether it is truly under-valued and likely to grow toward its true value. If it looks like a dog and smells like a dog (its low price accurately reflects its low value), then this stock is likely to send you barking up the wrong tree.

Of course, those undiscovered gems do exist. A stock may lose favor temporarily due to an economic blip, lagging sales, or an unexpected hit. Maybe a change in leadership sends investors running scared, or a new product proved to be a disappointment. Sometimes the company bounces back. Find out what's affecting the price.

Look on-line at the fifty-two-week high and low lists. These lists will give you a stock's track record. Many people say market investing is just like gambling. If you were betting at the race track, you'd look at the recent performance of the horses. Some initially burst from the gate, but can't go the distance. If the company shows up on the fifty-two-week low list, it's circling the drain, and you should probably avoid it. Choose companies with a steady history of growth or, at the very least, sustainability.

Is a stock with a high yield a good choice?

The dividend checks might be tempting, but don't use them as the sole indicator of a company's value. Dividends come from the company's cash, which is generated by earnings. While generous dividends might be a sign of financial growth, you should ask whether the company should be retaining its monies and reinvesting in the business—for expansion or acquisition, perhaps, that could lead to greater profitability for shareholders.

You should also remind yourself how the yield is calculated. The annual per-share dividend is divided by the per-share stock price. Let's say you bought a stock at forty dollars per share and were paid an annual dividend of one dollar; that's a 2.5 percent yield. Then the stock drops to thirty dollars a share, but the dividend remains the same. The yield goes up to 3.3 percent even though the value of the stock dropped. So, in this case, the high-yield figure is deceiving.

Companies aren't required to pay dividends. Many reinvest the money to keep the cash flow to continue building the company.

This doesn't mean you should ignore high-yield stocks, just that you should understand what drives that number. Also consider the tax consequences with any dividend.

When is the right time to bail out on a stock that's dropping?

Stock prices rise and fall, depending on many factors that we've discussed. Jumpy investors may react to downturns by anxiously selling and cutting their losses. Others look beneath these numbers to see if they can discover what's causing the drop. If it appears to be temporary, they ride it out. In some cases the stock will rebound and actually rise above the original value. At other times it keeps sinking like the *Titanic*.

Some traders make decisions by calculating a stock's pivot point. The pivot point takes an average of the previous day's activity for a stock. Add the high, low, and closing prices of the stock and divide by three. If the stock starts dipping below this point—say, by 7 percent or 8 percent—you can be fairly certain it's time to sell. Studies have shown that below this point, few stocks make a significant rebound.

How long do you stick with a winner?

It's hardest to decide to sell a stock when you see the price climbing. You're hearing the *ka-ching* of dollars resonating in your head and become dizzy with the dreams of untold wealth.

Here's a little advice: Snap out of it!

Don't get too greedy when a stock is making a vertical rise, particularly over a short period of time, like a week or two. A company cannot sustain that growth for long. When you're driving up a steep hill, you can see only the upward rise. But at some point this mountain is going to level off and may drop as radically as it rose. Do you want to cling to your stock in hopes of a yet higher peak, or should you sell before the upward incline starts tipping the other way? Once that happens, the market will be flooded with shares, the price will drop, and your profits may vanish. A "stop" order can be used to sell a stock if it drops to a certain price. If the stock price keeps climbing, your sell order doesn't execute. You can always move up the stop order as the price increases.

What are the risks and rewards of small cap stocks?

Some investors overlook small cap stocks because of the companies' size limitations. Small caps are, by definition, valued at $250 million to $2 billion. Doesn't sound so small, does it? When you consider that IBM has a cap of about $130.6 billion and Microsoft's cap is reaching $280 billion,[5] these small caps are indeed the little fishes in the stock ocean.

But small cap stocks might belong in your portfolio, because small companies have greater growth potential, and historically have outperformed large cap stocks, international stocks, bonds, CDs, and inflation. A small company is more likely to surge ahead with a 50-percent spurt than one of the giants. And remember that all those large-cap companies came into the world as small caps.

Another advantage of the small cap stocks is the restrictions placed on mutual funds that make it difficult for them to get in on these prospects. A fund manager is looking to invest millions of dollars in a company, to buy enough stock to make a difference in the fund's performance. Smaller companies can't support this large an investment. As a result, you, the individual investor, have first shot at what might become one of tomorrow's big success stories.

The other group that's missing out on small caps is the market analysts. Their focus is on the bigger players in the market, so they're not reporting on smaller companies. Without this scrutiny, the small cap stocks are sometimes under-priced, and therefore a great buy.

Now the downside. Everything I just wrote might not happen. Small caps are risky. They can sink just as easily as they can soar. They're the little fish, which means they can be devoured by the bigger predators. And because analysts aren't reporting on the small caps, you have to dig deeper to get the information you need to track them.

Be aware of small caps and don't cross them off your list too quickly. At the same time, know what you're getting into. Understand the nature of each business and its volatility. Look at the management. Is it spearheaded by a visionary entrepreneur who's not able to sustain the day-to-day management in the long run? Has it uncovered a cutting-edge niche that's likely to break out? As with any investment, decide your comfort level with the risk before making the purchase.

DEMYSTIFYING COMMODITIES

The commodities, or futures, market can be traced back to Chicago in the mid-nineteenth century. The McCormick Reaper Company started in 1848, and the new harvesting machine immediately began boosting wheat production. The city was a growing commercial center, linked to the east by railroad and telegraph lines. Midwest farmers brought their wheat harvests to Chicago to sell them to dealers who then shipped the wheat to their customers around the country. Farmers entered into contracts with dealers, guaranteeing their future harvests in exchange for cash. These contracts could move around a bit. One dealer might sell a contract to another. A farmer who couldn't deliver his wheat could pass the contract along to another farmer. When bad weather damaged crops, the remaining supply became more valuable. In more bountiful seasons, the reverse occurred. Speculators spotted the opportunity to buy contracts at a lower price and sell them for a profit if they could anticipate positive shifts.

Today's futures market maintains the same underlying approach. It's a guessing game. Unlike stocks, which you can hold as long as you want, commodities have a limited lifespan. The futures contract has an expiration date. Once the oranges, soybeans, or corn are harvested, the volume (the supply) and the demand determine the cost.

Is this a smart choice for me?

Commodities trading moves at a blistering speed. It isn't for the novice or casual trader. The intricacies of futures contracts, understanding the forecasts, and being aware of conditions that can impact the numbers might best be left to a specialist. A commodities broker regularly analyzes political shifts, natural disasters, and psychological factors that can push prices up or down in an instant. She charts the movement to identify patterns that prompt her to buy or sell. Success in this market demands intense and relentless scrutiny.

How do I find a broker who specializes in commodities?

Commodities brokers are like stockbrokers. They're licensed to buy and sell futures contracts. You can search on-line for a brokerage firm and, as with stocks, there are discount houses that offer limited services for lower fees. Look for a broker with at least five years of experience in commodities trading, and look at his track record.

You might hear the term "introducing broker." The IB can perform the same functions as a commodities broker—buy and sell—but cannot take money from a customer. The actual buying and selling is done by a Futures Commission Merchant (FCM) who handles the trading on the floor of the exchange while the IB works closely with you, the client. The intense demands of trading almost require the separation of duties.

ABOUT MUTUAL FUNDS

"Mutual fund" is a bit of a misnomer. The fund isn't just a bundle of stocks and bonds, but an investment company that manages a group of securities, presented to the investor as one entity. A mutual fund allows you to pool your resources with those of the other investors, diversifying your portfolio at a lower cost than if you attempted to purchase shares of each investment on your own. A professional fund manager or team oversees the fund and reports to the shareholders.

As an investor, you purchase shares in the entire fund; you can't pick and choose the individual securities. But each fund has its own strategy for choosing securities targeted at a particular objective; risk levels vary, depending on that goal. If you're looking for a higher return and are willing to experience more volatility (translation: You like roller coaster rides), choose a fund with a more aggressive investment strategy. Your financial adviser can help you identify the strategies and objectives of various mutual funds.

What's the difference between a mutual fund and a stock?

A stock may or may not be one component in a mutual fund. A mutual fund manages a portfolio of various investments: stocks, bonds, short-term money market instruments, other securities, or assets, or any combination.

What's the advantage of investing in a mutual fund?

By pooling your money with that of other investors, a mutual fund offers you the opportunity to diversify your portfolio with a smaller investment. The mutual fund is managed by a professional investment adviser who's registered with the Securities and Exchange Commission, so you also benefit from the experience of a knowledgeable specialist overseeing your investments. You also enjoy liquidity, since you can redeem your shares at any time, although you may have to pay fees for doing so, as well as income tax on any disbursements.

A mutual fund has its drawbacks. You're one step removed from control of your investments, because you aren't directly involved with the securities in your fund. When you invest in a particular stock, you can monitor its activity by checking the website. Tracking a mutual fund is more complicated, but certainly not an insurmountable task if you're willing to put forth the effort.

Finally, mutual funds are notorious for piling up the fees. You don't get that professional management for nothing! Although there are several classes of mutual funds and they all operate differently, you might pay a sales charge (known as a "load") when you buy or sell shares. This fee goes to the broker who handles the transaction. You may also pay a purchase fee when you buy shares and a redemption fee when you sell them. You might pay an exchange fee for exchanging shares from one fund to another in the same fund "family." Some funds also charge an account fee to offset maintenance costs. There can also be management fees, distribution fees—the list goes on.

These costs can nibble away at your investment until a big bite is missing. According to the SEC website (sec.gov), if you invested $10,000 in a mutual fund that delivered a 10 percent annual return before expenses and posted 1.5 percent annual operating expenses, after twenty years, your investment would be about $49,725. If the fund's expenses were one point less—.5 percent—you would have $60,858. That's 22.4 percent more money with a 1 percent drop in operating costs. So, a little number can make a big difference.

Be sure you understand the extra charges involved before you invest in a fund, so your hard-earned money doesn't trickle into fees that deliver no value to you.

Are mutual funds a safer investment than stocks?

Different funds have different risks. Money market funds, for example, offer very low risk. But risk and reward are closely related, and a money market fund generally delivers lower returns than bond or stock funds. Such a cautious investment might not keep pace with inflation.

Bond funds aren't as restrictive as money market funds. The SEC doesn't limit bond funds to high-quality or short-term investments, as they do with money markets. So this option kicks your risk and your reward potential up a notch.

Stocks included in a mutual fund represent the same risk here as they do when you're investing in them on your own. The upside is that you'll be better diversified to lessen that risk, assuming you have a good fund manager. Whether you purchase stocks yourself or as part of a mutual fund, in the long run this investment may deliver the strongest returns.

How do I choose a mutual fund?

Some funds are more aggressive, seeking to deliver higher yields. Other funds are more mainstream. Discuss with your investment adviser your financial goals, both short- and long-term, to determine which fund best matches your needs and investment style. Every mutual fund has a prospectus and shareholder's report. You should review both documents before investing. In the prospectus, check the risk/return bar chart to see the fund's annual total returns for each of the past ten years. Review the costs listed in the fee table. Look at the financial highlights listed in the prospectus, with audited reports of the fund's performance for each of the previous five years. The shareholder's report lists the securities currently in the fund, so you can see where your investment is going.

LOOKING AT BONDS

Bonds are probably the most overlooked and misunderstood investment among newcomers. Many people associate bonds with those U.S. savings bonds, and compared to the excitement and dynamics of the stock market, they seem like a dull alternative. In reality, bonds belong in just about everyone's portfolio, from the new college grad to the senior citizen.

A bond is a loan you make to the organization that issues it (the "issuer"). For this reason, a bond is a debt, while stock is considered equity. In return for your investment, you receive a predetermined amount of interest. The higher the risk, the greater the interest rate. A bond issued by a government or municipality offers a lower interest because of the higher likelihood that your debt will be repaid. When a corporation issues a bond, the interest rate (the "coupon") reflects the credit risk. A blue chip corporation issuing a bond will give a lower coupon than a company with less stellar credit. You can check out a company's credit risk by looking at its bond rating. This is like a report card, issued by ratings agencies like Standard and Poor, Moody's, and Fitch. The ratings range from AAA for the highest quality to C or D, which indicates that the company is in default. It's also important to point out that government and municipal bonds are tax advantaged where corporate bonds are not.

Terms

The *coupon* refers to the interest rate, harkening back to the days when a bondholder would receive a booklet of coupons that could be torn out and redeemed for interest payments.

Maturity indicates when the term of the bond ends and the principal will be repaid.

Par value is the amount of money a bond holder will receive when the bond matures. Also known as "face value," the par isn't the same as the actual price of the bond, since that amount may vary between purchase and maturity. For example, if interest rates are higher than the bond's coupon rate, then the bond is sold below par or at a discount. But if interest rates are lower than the bond's coupon rate, then the bond is sold at a premium, also known as above par.

Yield is derived by dividing the dollar value of the coupon by the par (face) value of the bond.

If I buy stocks, why would I want bonds?

Quite simply, bonds diversify your portfolio. In general, a bond is predictable and provides balance, particularly during a sluggish stock market. With the maturity dates, you can manage your short-term investments, knowing how much income to expect and when. As you near retirement age, bonds offer a better guarantee of retirement income than stocks. If you're looking to save for a college education, a bond offers lower risk than stocks and higher return than a traditional savings account.

Why do some businesses offer bonds rather than stock?

When a business needs to raise capital—for expansion, to acquire another business, for example—it has several options. The company can go to the bank for a loan, but a large corporation may need more money than a bank can lend. The company can offer stock, if it's a publicly held business. The stockholders became partial owners, which means the business owners are giving up some control. If the company is privately owned, it would have to go through a lengthy process called an initial public offering (IPO) before it can sell stock. By offering bonds, a business is borrowing money from investors and repaying the interest only until the bond matures. Bonds are debts that need to be repaid, but at least the business owner maintains control.

How do I make money from a bond?

When you purchase a bond, you're loaning the par or face value. The coupon states how much interest you'll be paid, and the debt must be repaid at the maturity date. During the period of the bond, you'll receive interest payments; when the bond matures, you'll be repaid the face value. For example, if you buy a bond worth $5,000 at 7 percent for ten years, you would receive

$350 a year for ten years, which means your $5,000 investment will give you a $3,500 profit over a ten-year period.

Are there different types of bonds?

Yes. Bonds come in all sizes and from various issuers, just as loans do, and each has its pros and cons. Take a look at some of your options to see which bonds make sense for your portfolio.

Government bonds. You've probably heard about "T-bills." They fall under this grouping. Marketable securities that are issued by the federal government are known as "Treasuries." They're classified according to the maturity term. A "bill" matures in less than a year; a "note" matures in one to ten years; and a "bond" matures in more than ten years. Government securities are the safest of any type of bond, because the government isn't likely to default, and you may also gain some tax benefits. For example, if you buy federal government bonds, you won't pay Uncle Sam, but you may be taxed at the state and local levels.

Municipal bonds. Also known as "munis," these are issued by state and local governments. The risk of a muni is only slightly higher than that of government bonds. Cities rarely go bankrupt, but it can happen. Munis may not offer a high interest rate, but they do feature one big plus: The returns are free from federal tax. In some cases, the local government sweetens the deal by making the bonds completely tax-free.

Corporate bonds. These bonds present a higher interest rate because the chance of a business defaulting is much greater. The amount of a corporate bond can vary greatly, depending on what the market can bear. The maturity of a corporate bond can be short-term (less than five years), intermediate (five to twelve years) or long-term (more than twelve years).

Corporate bonds come in different configurations. A *convertible bond*, for example, can be converted to stock. A *zero-coupon bond* offers no interest payments (coupons) during the term but sells at a price below par value. This means you could potentially purchase a $1,000 ten-year bond for $600. A *callable bond* is a security that can be "called back" by the issuer before the bond matures. Before you invest in any corporate bond, check the company's bond rating to see what kind of risk you're taking.

What is a junk bond?

Probably the most common term associated with bonds is "junk." Junk bonds are like any other bond in that they're loans you make to a business with a defined maturity date and coupon. What sets a junk bond apart from the others is the credit rating of the issuer, as provided by S&P, Moody's, and Fitch. Companies with a rating of AAA to BBB are considered investment grade. When they slip below this mark—to between a BB and D—they're noted as somewhere between "speculative" and "in default," respectively, and they're listed as "junk" grade. That's a harsh word and may not always indicate the issuer's situation. A company might be bouncing back from a bad credit rating and on its way to full recovery, but hasn't yet climbed out of the junk grade. These issuers are called "rising stars." Then you have the "fallen angels," which are sliding downward and are likely to drag you with them.

The added risk boosts the yield on junk bonds, and sometimes it's worth taking a shot. Sometimes. Before you buy a junk bond, compare the yield to a Treasury (government bond). If it's greater than six percent, the junk bond might be worth the investment. You should also know that if the issuer goes bankrupt, a bondholder is in a better position than a stockholder. Since a bond is a debt, bondholders are higher on the list to be repaid, even if it's only a fraction of the par value, while a stockholder could end up with nothing.

Are there other risks involved with bonds?

A bond is a relatively safe investment but, of course, there are caveats. As with any opportunity to make money, a few features of bonds can affect your return.

The price can change. If you loan someone $1,000, how can the amount change? The par value (the amount you're loaning) isn't the same as the price of the bond. The price is what the bond is worth on the market, if you're looking to buy or sell. A bond's price is affected by its yield, which is calculated by dividing the coupon by the par value. Stay with me. If you have a $1,000 bond with a 10 percent ($100) coupon, the yield is 10 percent ($100/$1,000). If the bond's price drops to $800, the yield goes up to 12.5 percent, because the coupon remains at $100. If the price increases to $1,200, the yield sinks to 8.33 percent. Fluctuating interest rates affect a bond's price, which, in turn, affects the yield.

The rate can change. You can purchase either a fixed-rate or floating-rate bond, for which the percentage of your coupon goes up and down through the term, according to market trends. If you anticipate an upswing in the market, a floating-rate bond can give you a better return, but you're taking a chance that rates can slide in the other direction. Also know that as interest rates rise in the marketplace, the prices of previously issued bonds will fall. On the other hand, in a market where interest rates are falling, the price of a previously issued bond could increase.

The issuer can call back the bond. We looked at callable bonds, which give the issuer the option of calling back the bond and cashing it in early. In this instance, you lose the remaining interest. These bonds might be called back because the issuer wants to take advantage of dropping interest rates, issuing new ones at the lower market rate. This becomes more likely if the rates drop a point or more below your coupon. Then you not only have lost the anticipated return, but you also might have difficulty finding an investment in current market conditions with a similar yield.

When you're considering a callable bond, look at two things—the call premium and call protection. A call premium is the issuer's payment to you if the bond is called back—the amount the company is willing to offer you for your risk. Call protection is the period during which the bond cannot be recalled, even if interest rates are dropping.

How long do I have to commit to a bond investment?

There's no set date. The maturity date of a bond is determined by the issuer. A bond's maturity can be as brief as one day or as long as one hundred years. Typically, a bond will mature in one to twenty years. The shorter the time span, the more predictable the investment—that is, the better able you are to gauge whether or not your loan will be repaid. So shorter bonds usually offer a lower interest rate, while longer term bonds, which can shift according to market conditions, generally give you a higher rate. Also, an investor is not required to hold a bond until maturity. It can always be sold in the secondary market if the bond is that of a reputable issuer.

What is laddering?

When you buy bonds, you may have to deal with having them called back. Laddering is the practice of buying bonds with different maturity dates so that the call protection is staggered. In this way, your investments are protected from a big loss if they were all to be called at the same time. Although callable bonds won't necessarily be called, laddering is a smart way to manage your bond portfolio.

How do I buy a bond?

As with stocks, you can buy your bonds through a broker—full-service or discount. A brokerage firm might require a steep minimum deposit to get started. If it's a little rich for your blood, ask about bond funds, which are managed like mutual funds. If available, a bond fund can give you diversification without a big investment.

Government bonds can often be purchased at your local bank or financial institution. You can also buy them on-line, directly from the government. Go to www.treasurydirect.gov for information. TreasuryDirect was established by the U.S. Bureau of Public Debt to allow buyers to purchase bonds without a broker and a broker's commissions.

When is the best time to sell a bond?

When interest rates are climbing, you might be able to sell above par. Keep an eye on interest rates. As we said before, a drop in rates could signal a call back on your bond if it's not under call protection or close to maturity. If you sell before a call, you could prevent a loss. You should also keep an eye on the stability of the issuer. Look for signs that the company is faltering, like the bond rating dropping. Bonds are like stocks; they change with the market. You need to watch your investment to maximize its potential.

THE MANY OPTIONS FOR RETIREMENT PLANS

Retirement plans present a wonderful opportunity to stash away money a little at a time for the golden years and earn a significant return. The difference between the various plans can be perplexing. This type of investment has more to do with navigating tax laws than watching market fluctuations. With a little knowledge and effort, you can build your retirement fund to provide the financial security you seek. Much more on this in chapter 8, but for now here are some of the basics.

Terms

A *qualified plan* is a retirement plan established and offered by an employer, but it's not an IRA-based plan. A qualified plan has different restrictions regarding contributions and distributions. Employers receive a tax deduction for amounts they contribute to the plan, and taxes on earnings for these funds are deferred. A 401(k) and an Employee Stock Ownership Plan are examples of qualified plans.

Rollover is reinvesting funds from one qualified tax-free plan to another to avoid paying penalties or taxes.

How do I choose a retirement plan?

Some employers offer a plan to employees as an added benefit, and you should take advantage of such a perk whenever you can. You're not limited to one retirement account. You can start others on your own. Check out the plans, the benefits, the restrictions, and the expected returns to determine how you can begin to invest in a future that's quickly creeping up on you.

Traditional IRA. If you'll be under the age of 70.5 on December 31 and are currently working (including self-employed), you qualify to open a Traditional IRA. You contribute a portion of your income (wages, salaries, bonuses, and commissions) up to a specified limit and will not pay taxes on that money until you withdraw it. There's no penalty if you leave the money in the account until you reach 59.5, become disabled, or suffer a financial hardship. If you don't touch it until you're retired, you'll also likely be taxed in a lower income bracket. You can open a Traditional IRA at any IRS-approved institution, including brokerage firms.

401(k). This qualified plan is offered by some employers as an employment benefit. An eligible employee makes voluntary pre-tax contributions to the account, and the employer makes matching or other contributions, such as profit-sharing. Income tax on the earnings is deferred until the employee withdraws money from the account. Only a limited percentage of your salary may be contributed each year.

SIMPLE IRA. It sounds easy, but in this case SIMPLE is an acronym for Savings Incentive Match Plan for Employees. The plan is designed for small businesses with a maximum of one hundred employees. As with the 401(k), this plan allows contributions by both the employee and employer. All contributions are pre-tax and grow deferred, until you withdraw it at retirement. The SIMPLE is easier to administer than most qualified plans.

SEP. The Simplified Employee Pension (SEP) is an IRA-based plan in which employers can make discretionary contributions, and employees are not allowed to contribute. Employees wishing to participate must have an established Traditional IRA in order to accept SEP contributions from an employer. This is usually set up for them. As with some retirement accounts, contributions and earnings in the SEP are tax-deferred.

Roth IRA. Established in 1997 and named for the late Senator William Roth, Jr., the Roth IRA has become perhaps the hottest retirement account, because participants contribute post-tax monies and therefore pay no additional taxes when funds are withdrawn. In other words, rather than taking the tax deduction while you're still working and can conceivably afford to pay the taxes, you take the tax hit now. Your earnings grow on a tax-deferred basis and can be withdrawn free of federal income taxes as long as you play by the rules. That means you must have a Roth IRA for at least five years, and you must be 59 ½ years old, or be disabled, or be paying for the purchase or construction of your first home ($10,000 lifetime maximum). Although the Roth IRA has income and contribution caps, there are no limits to the number of IRA accounts you can have as long as you don't go over total dollar contribution limits.

Roth 401(k). Brand new in 2006, this hybrid account blends the tax-free advantage of a Roth IRA with the 401(k) qualified plan. Contributions from the employee are already taxed, a feature that the government likes since it doesn't have to wait to collect. But unlike the Roth plan that spawned it, this offspring has no income limitations.

403(b). This tax-sheltered annuity plan is another employer-administered retirement fund, like a 401(k) plan, but is available only to certain employees of public schools and tax-exempt organizations and some ministries. Tax-deferred contributions are voluntary, and the plan has income limits.

529. This state-sponsored education savings plan was created under Section 529 of the IRS Code and is available only in certain states. In some cases, either the purchaser or the beneficiary of the plan must be a resident of the state, but not all plans require this. If it's available where you live, the 529 allows tax-deferred contributions, and earnings are distributed tax-free when used to pay qualified higher education expenses. You can open a 529 for your child, grandchild, relative, friend, or even yourself, and anyone can make a contribution to the fund. Individuals can contribute up to $11,000 annually.

Coverdell Education Savings Account. Formerly known as an Education IRA, this fund is similar to a 529, although total annual contributions are limited to $2,000. Contributors who meet the fund's income guidelines can take advantage of the same tax-free distributions as in the 529, when used for qualified elementary, secondary, or higher education expenses. The Coverdell is a good option in states where the 529 is not available. Check residency requirements on these as well.

How do I open an IRA?

For an employer-sponsored account (such as a SIMPLE IRA or SEP IRA), talk to your Human Resources Director about eligibility and enrollment. Ask about contribution limitations and the employer's policy on matching funds. You can open traditional or Roth IRAs through an IRS-approved financial institution or brokerage.

Can I withdraw money from a retirement account before I retire?
In most cases you can withdraw money early but will be assessed a 10% penalty by the IRS. In addition, you'll be required to pay the income taxes on that amount, either at the time you make the withdrawal or on your income tax return for that year. Some plans allow you to take a loan against a portion of your balance and effectively pay yourself back with interest, but I don't advise this. Try to keep this account intact for retirement.

CERTIFICATES OF DEPOSIT

Parked unobtrusively in the crowded lot of investment opportunities is the certificate of deposit. A CD is also known as a time deposit and is literally "money in the bank." A CD is an agreement with a financial institution, guaranteeing a specified rate of interest for a minimum deposit for a set amount of time. With a CD you deposit the money and wait, so many investors seek other more adventuresome investments. But there's an appropriate time for CDs, if only to enter into investments.

Why should I buy one?
A CD offers a risk-free, short-term investment. Because the deposit is FDIC-insured, you're guaranteed to get back at least what you put into the CD. And CDs can be purchased for periods as short as three months, so it's a safe way to make your money work for you when you can't spare the cash for long. The disadvantage of CD investment, especially in recent years, is that after taxes and inflation are considered, a CD with a low rate may not really help advance you towards your goals.

How much can I deposit?

CDs usually require a minimum of about $1000, and FDIC insures your deposit up to $100,000.

Can I withdraw my money before the term ends?

With a few exceptions, there's usually a penalty for making early withdrawals from a CD. You've deposited the money so that the financial institution can invest it to make more money; withdrawing funds too soon is like breaking your promise. Read the contract carefully to know your obligations, and only deposit money that you can part with for the specified period.

FIVE COMMON INVESTMENT MISTAKES

You should be aware of some mistakes novices (and seasoned investors) often make.

Overestimating risk tolerance. If you find yourself losing sleep because of some of your more aggressive investments, sit down with a financial adviser and identify the boundaries of your financial comfort zone.

Impatience. Successful investing—particularly in stocks—requires commitment. Don't invest in a security and expect to become an instant millionaire. You need to be able to stick with your investments, even through the lows, to make the most of them.

Buying from the heart. Don't let your emotions about a stock cloud your judgment about its fiscal value. If you feel good about a cause, make a donation. If you really like a product, stock up on it, but not on the stock—until you've made sure it's a sound investment.

Insufficient research. Dig around for the measures of a stock's worthiness that we've discussed. Talk to a financial adviser. Ask the dumb questions. An educated decision is the best way to avoid investment mistakes.

Poor diversification. It's human nature to stay where you feel comfortable, but when it comes to investments, spread out. Look for varying risk levels to cushion your portfolio against a painful hit. A portfolio that invests in many areas of the market (bonds, large cap stocks, small caps, international stocks, and money markets) actually has less risk than a portfolio invested in only one area of the market.

ONE LAST WORD ABOUT INVESTING

If you think you don't have enough money to begin investing, you just haven't looked hard enough. For as little as a few hundred dollars, you can start building a portfolio. Every day that you procrastinate about investing, someone else is making money that should have been yours. Now that you're armed with the information to join the investment community, put your knowledge—and your money—to good use.

CHAPTER FIVE

Creating Your Own Business

She makes linen garments and sells them,
and supplies belts to the tradesmen.

PROVERBS 31:24

Years of interviewing business owners on television news and on radio through the National Association of Women Business Owners has shown me many different business models—from buying into an existing system (like a franchise), to joining a multilevel marketing company, to starting from scratch. The latter approach is the focus of this chapter because it's the most difficult. The one thing I've heard again and again is that you have to organize your time, particularly by separating business from home life. In other words, as a successful Mary Kay representative told me, you can't do your laundry and your business at the same time.

This chapter includes practical advice and experiences I've gleaned from highly successful business owners, some of it based on opinions (theirs and mine), which may vary from yours. The point is not total agreement, but to get you thinking about your own goals and preferences as you consider your field.

Am I ready to be a business owner?

Building a business is a great adventure, but every adventure has its risks. However, you can mitigate some of the risk by planning ahead, researching the market for your products or services, and evaluating how much you know in your area of business.

The founder of a highly successful home-based baby products company—and father of twin newborns—became an expert on baby products virtually overnight. The demands of parenting twins convinced him that a home-based business made the most sense for his family, so he decided to take the chance and try to leverage his newfound knowledge. From the beginning he was armed with crucial insight into the behavior of his target market—where they shopped, what magazines they read and which websites they visited. He knew exactly how to position his business, and where to begin advertising it. Why? Because he knew there was a real need for the convenience of "one-stop shopping" in the twins' community. Harried new parents didn't have the time to scour the web and would gladly take recommendations and buy products from someone in a similar situation.

In recent years, many new business owners have jumped on the eBay bandwagon just because they got a great wholesale deal on a load of products. But having no real interest in or knowledge of what they were selling, their customer service almost always suffered. Since the primary goal was to simply "move product," these businesses tended to have a fly-by-night quality that was obvious to customers and wholesalers. If you can't answer your customers' questions knowledgably, they'll simply find another merchant who can! Taking an inventory of your personal knowledge base and skill set right now can mean the difference between success and failure. Stick with what you know. Honestly reflect on your abilities, and commit to learning something new if necessary.

Fortunately, excellent resources are available to small business owners. Consider starting with the Small Business Administration, whose website, www.sba.gov, has excellent information about developing business plans, and contains links to training and other resources. To exchange information with an on-line community of small business owners, visit www.smallbusinessbrief.com. If you live in a metropolitan area, you might also consider making an appointment with SCORE, the Service Corps of Retired Executives (www.score.org). They offer a number of services ranging from getting funding to seeking legal advice. They accept payment on a sliding scale and sometimes offer their services free of charge.

Another common misconception is that owning a business will give you lots of extra free time. In reality you'll probably put in extra hours to make your business work and to deal with the unexpected. The most successful home-based business owners I've talked to all shared a singular passion for their work and the multitude of challenges associated with it. The majority just liked what they did and didn't watch the clock. Successful business owners thrive on the challenge of building a customer base, prospecting, offering new products, and experimenting with different advertising methods.

If you have a clear idea of your personal and business goals, you're closer to being ready to start your business. Goals allow us to think about lifestyle priorities. Write down the things that motivated you to consider a home business—more time with family, increased independence, a better income, and so on.

How can I draw boundaries between work and home life?

For a home-based business, start by thinking about your home's physical structure. While a completely separate room with a door is ideal to diminish distractions, any effort you can put into dedicating a portion of a room to work-related activities will help.

Then consider your attitude. If you find yourself craving the structure of your old nine-to-five job, or keep sneaking away from your desk to do the dishes or to answer the house phone, tell yourself you're "going to the office" and act accordingly. Get up at the same time you used to for work, take a shower, and put on dressier work clothes. This will get you into a mindset to distinguish between your home and the separate, professional workspace within it.

Is it time to quit my full-time job?

Starting a business is like planting a tree. You have to give it a good solid foundation—your time, effort, and money—before it will grow and flourish. You can't just wake up one morning and quit your job if you don't have your home business in place, organized, and already generating enough sales to support your needs. Your full-time job provides a stable income and benefits while you're building your home business. Translation: Less stress about money! This frees you to focus more on marketing, pleasing your customer, and finding your niche without worrying about how you're going to feed your family. Besides, if your business doesn't work out, you're still employed!

Keeping your full-time job reduces the amount of debt you'll need to start your business. It's best to finance your home business needs from your personal savings. The less you borrow from the bank, the less you put on the credit card, and the less you have to pay for debt during your start-up period, the stronger your business's foundation in the long run.

When does a hobby become a business?

How about baking a pretzel and turning it into a multimillion-dollar business? That's what Anne Beiler did, turning something she loved—baking—into Auntie Anne's, Inc. Many businesses start as hobbies, maybe even the thing you loved to do as a kid. You can earn income by making crafts, fixing things, designing greeting cards, caring for children, cleaning houses, landscaping, and thousands of other pursuits.

Are people asking you to make or do something for them? Start making appointments with them to discuss business arrangements. Who knows? You may become the next Auntie Anne or Mrs. Fields.

What type of business should I create?

There are four basic types of business structures: the sole proprietorship, the partnership, the unincorporated structure like an LLC and LLP (Limited Liability Company or Partnership), and the corporation. In a *sole proprietorship* you're the only owner and you make all the decisions. You sign all the checks, and you set the goals for fulfilling the business idea that you created. The downside: You also take on all of the liability. A *partnership* involves two or more people who own and direct the business. Each partner also gets a share of the revenue. In the home business setting, a partnership is often a husband and wife, sisters, brothers, or family members. Again, you personally share the liability.

The *limited liability company* can be one, two, or several people—known as "members"—who own and direct the business. This is my favorite business structure for owning and operating real estate, because your personal assets are protected. If you're running a risky business—one in which someone can sue you or your employees could be hurt—you should consider an LLC. If something happens, only your business assets are on the line, not your personal assets. No structure is perfect, but your home, your personal savings, and your personal liability should remain untouchable. Your lawyer can set up an LLC for you. It usually costs less than $500 to file the necessary paperwork with the city courthouse and with the IRS.

Corporations are usually thought to be huge businesses with twenty-story office buildings, but they can be small businesses as well. Your lawyer can set up either a C corporation or an S corporation for your business needs, and it will cost you only about $500 to file all the paperwork. C corporations have three levels of authority—shareholders, a board of directors, and officers.

These structures can issue stock, and the number of shareholders is generally unrestricted. C corporations can issue two types of shares—preferred (which are paid back first if the practice is liquidated) and common shares. The major downside of C corporations is that profits are taxed twice—first at the corporate level and again when the shareholders receive their cut.

An S corporation can also issue stock, but it's limited to seventy-five shareholders, and it can't issue both common and preferred shares of stock. The biggest advantage of S corporations is that profits can flow directly to the owners' personal tax returns. Because of this, an S corporation's profits avoid the double tax whammy. There are also different rules governing how an owner takes money from a corporation and how to pay taxes on it.

Business owners must keep careful accounting records for all types of businesses. See your accountant for more on choosing the best business structure for you.

How do I choose a name for my business?

A business name is important for the overall look, feel, and marketing of your business. Your business name should reflect what your business is about, and it should be memorable. If you're selling hats and purses, you might call your business "Sheila's Outlandish Hats" or "Sheila's Home of Hats." A wonderful woman I once interviewed has made a living teaching people the art of giving gifts. (Talk about taking a hobby and making it profitable!) Her business name is Think Thoughtful, Inc. You want to keep your business name unique, something that will catch the buyer's eye. Set yourself apart from the rest. Brand your name, and don't try to make it similar to a big business chain; that will only scream "knock off."

Use your business name on everything you sell, on invoices, on your answering machine, on your letterhead, and, of course, in advertising. You might even pay a graphic artist to develop a logo for your business. Many people remember pictures better than names, and a logo helps create a stronger impression in your customers' eyes.

What about getting a tax identification number?

Anyone going into business needs a tax identification number, which serves the same purpose for your business as your social security number does for you personally. Everyone from suppliers to banks is going to want it. Without one, you'll have to give out your personal social security number. Bad idea. A tax identification number protects your personal information from identity theft, and it appears more professional when seeking credit lines or when you're dealing business to business. Perhaps even more importantly, using a tax identification number protects your personal credit from being overextended.

Applying for a tax identification number on-line is easy. Just head over to www.irs.gov and type in "EIN number" in the search field. You can print out the application, or you can fill it out on-line. Even if you won't have employees, a tax identification number will make your business complete in the eyes of banks and the IRS. Having a tax identification number doesn't increase the taxes you owe; taxes for a business are based on its income and circumstances.

What does it cost to start a business?

Starting any business will involve some amount of money right from the beginning. The amount will depend on your personal situation, the type of business you're starting, and the resources you already have. It's important to plan your financial needs before you jump into action. I recommend saving by automatic deduction with your employer until you have enough to lay a firm foundation. I strongly believe in building your business slowly; taking a year or two to save money is wise in building a company that could support you for a lifetime.

The first cost to consider is your personal needs—like rent or mortgage payment, utilities, groceries, doctor bills, maintenance and insurance for your vehicles, and clothing. If those costs are low, or if you have a job that you can rely on for now, your business won't have to support your personal needs. If you don't have a "day job" or any type of savings, consider getting a temporary job. Otherwise you may struggle for a few months, until your business is profitable enough to generate money for business expenses and your personal upkeep.

Scrimping on personal extras—like entertainment, eating out, and home decorations—in order to make it through the first six months is important. Try to have a plan for paying the bills; if you're constantly worried about paying for car insurance, the sitter, medical bills, or food, you might start to think that your business isn't worth it. But it is!

Now for the up-front business costs. Expenses will vary depending on the type of company you're opening. For instance, some businesses can function out of your home, while others will need warehouse space, an office building, or a storefront immediately. If you hire employees, you may have to set up policies for workman's compensation or other liability and health insurance policies. You'll need materials for your product, you might need machines, or you may need one or two delivery vehicles. Here are just a few possible up-front needs:

- rent or mortgage for a building
- property insurance, utilities, janitorial services, or maintenance for a building
- business license fees and local business taxes
- computers
- accounting software
- office furniture

- lawyer or accountant fees
- marketing supplies (business cards, fliers, letterhead)
- uniforms
- phone service and cell phones
- Internet service
- employee insurance

Sit down and list everything you need. Take your time; try to think of every little detail. Then research average prices for each item so you can get an idea of your total up-front costs. Your research may turn up cheaper alternatives, so it pays to do your homework!

Why is it so important to set flexible goals for my business?

From long before your first sale, throughout the life of your business, one of your most important activities is to set flexible goals. A goal is simply the end result you'd like to see. Goals give you direction and help you make daily decisions. With each decision ask yourself, "Will this help me achieve my goals?" When obstacles get in your way, goals help you get back on your feet and keep marching toward the finish line.

Once you have a goal, make a step-by-step plan for getting there. How will you find customers? Where will you purchase materials? How will you grow your company? Write your goals and your plans on paper so you can remember them and stay focused.

Some possible goals:

- Establish an organized office space with the necessary equipment and furniture.
- Set up a business checking account.
- Obtain a business identification number and set up business accounting software.

- Find trustworthy suppliers.
- Find an affordable and timely shipping method.
- Create a website for on-line marketing.
- Sell enough product or service to make an overall 10 percent profit by the end of the second year.
- Increase sales by 20 percent each year.

Goals can range from tasks to accomplish to long-term results you want to see. Make long-term goals specific and easy to measure, so you'll know whether or not you're achieving them. Sit back regularly and review your goals. Did you meet some? Did you fall short? Don't beat yourself up if you don't hit every mark. Who does when first starting out? What new goals do you have? If you don't set new written business goals at least once a year, your business will likely stop growing.

What is the best way to get organized?

When you start up an office, you need to become organized and functional. As I write this, I'm looking around my home office at piles of paper to file. (I'll get to it after I write this chapter.) Make sure you can access everything easily. When a client calls or visits your office, it's important to be able to find the needed materials quickly and efficiently.

Boring though it may be, filing is an important part of your business organization. Get a few filing cabinets—as many as you can fit in your office. Having enough space to keep your business information safe and organized will help you function efficiently. You may want to order your files alphabetically, by category, or by date—whatever works best for you. Label each drawer and each file for easy retrieval. A few empty drawers won't hurt. Remember, your company will grow!

A locking cabinet or fire-proof safe comes in handy for most offices. These keep money or confidential documents safe from strangers, curious employees, or in some cases, natural disasters like floods or fires. Don't take any chances with your company and its success.

Keep a close eye on all the important supplies that your business demands. Keep an updated inventory so that you can reorder when you're running low. Organize your supplies in a closet or cabinet so that you can see what you have. Ordering items that you already have wastes important company money.

Try to keep a log of important phone calls. You may need this when you're looking for a phone number, or it might help you remember something you promised to do. Integrity is everything in business.

Should I borrow money for my business?

Ah, here's a tough one. Wouldn't it be wonderful if we all had enough money saved to begin our business? Often that's not the case. This is where the contrast between good debt and bad debt comes in. Bad debt includes credit card debt, department store cards, and financing that vacation to Disney World. Good debt eventually helps put money in your pocket and build your assets—including your business.

If I decide to get a business loan, how do I start?

All kinds of loans are available for most business opportunities, including small business loans. You can also get help from the government. Most business loans come with decent interest rates and special features. You can also apply for lines of credit, but use these with caution and be wary of overextending yourself. Many people find themselves in trouble or bankruptcy because they couldn't manage their credit.

Many business ideas have higher-than-average startup costs. For these, getting a bank loan may involve extra work. First do your research. Get as much information as you can on all the banks that are willing to lend you business money. This may include banks in your area and banks that are out of town or even in another state. Take your time and find the best deal. Talk with an account representative in person or by phone, or research a bank's loan programs on-line. Some lenders are developing better and more secure websites, but on-line you aren't able to speak to an individual.

Make sure you're prepared before submitting your application. Banks may have different requirements. Your lender will tell you whether you need one or more of the following things:

- a business plan
- a cosigner for the loan
- collateral
- tax and income records
- a tax identification number
- your business name
- a checking account
- proof of sales

A business plan is a written set of goals for the business. The bank uses this to understand your business—where you'll sell, how much you can sell, your source of income for repayment, what your competition is selling, and the business's future outlook. When preparing your business plan, list your goals, what personal assets you're going to put into the business, and your expected long-term business results. A business plan can be formal (prepared by a professional) or informal (written by you). If you need a formal business plan, your local small business administration office will help you put together a plan free of charge. Software programs are also available that make this process easy and produce a professional-looking document.

You may need a cosigner for your business loan. If so, make sure it's someone with a good credit history. This will make the application process easier.

Collateral for a business loan can be any type of asset that the bank can confiscate if you don't repay the full amount of the loan. This may include your home, car, or business equipment. Be careful how much you borrow, and plan carefully how you will pay it back in a reasonable amount of time.

How do I open a business bank account?

It's essential to have a separate business checking account, from which to pay your employees and business expenses. It's smart also to set up a business savings account and ideally to turn it into an interest-bearing account (like a money market). This allows you to build up business profits and make money on the cash that's sitting there. Most banks have special checking and savings rates for businesses. You should definitely shop around to see what banks or credit unions have to offer your company. Avoid unnecessary fees, and make sure you have easy access to your account information, preferably on-line. Ask your bank manager about fraud protection—a must-have for good business management.

Customer service and availability are important. You need a dependable account manager as your main contact. This person (or team at larger banks) should also be capable of helping you make future investments to maximize your profit and company growth.

How should I handle accounting for my business?

Every type of business needs some method of accounting to track your gross income (your sales) and your expenses. Sales minus expenses equals your net income—information you need for tax purposes, to decide how much to put back into the business for expansion, or for purchasing additional materials. Your income level also indicates how well your business is doing overall. Accounting systems can help you analyze spending trends, stick to a budget, and make important financial decisions.

If you don't need a computer for any type of sales, marketing, or communication in the business, you can keep all your accounting functions on paper, but it will take much more time than you might think. Nonetheless, you can find journals and notebooks for tracking all your expenses and sales in any local office supply store. This is still my husband's method of handling his business. I have yet to bring him into the on-line banking age.

I find it much simpler to use a computer. You can use a basic spreadsheet, or you can purchase accounting software, like Quicken, QuickBooks, or Microsoft Money. Accounting software doesn't have to be expensive, and you can find many types in the local office supply store, or wherever computers and software are sold. Accounting software and services are also available on-line. Some on-line companies will even pay your bills, pay your employees, and prepare your taxes. That scares me a bit, but choose the option that works best for you. Do small chunks of your accounting work daily or weekly so you won't be stuck sorting through a huge box of receipts at the end of the year.

How am I paid as a business owner?

This is where I don't make a move without my CPA. It's wise to seek an accountant's advice before you try to take money from your business for yourself. Rules for this differ, depending on the type of business. Also keep your bottom line in mind. You may have to wait to take income from your business until it has enough sales coming in to cover expenses and make a profit. And be careful not to take out so much that you make any outstanding checks bounce!

One of the easiest methods for an owner to take money from a business is through an "owner withdrawal," which comes as a check written to you each week or month. If you have an LLC or a corporation, you can take money from the business in the form of a weekly, biweekly, or monthly paycheck. In any case, these checks must be entered into your accounting system, and you should consult with your accountant about handling the taxes for that type of income. Each state has different laws governing your payment methods, so work with your accountant to stay in compliance.

Who are my customers?

In order to start any business, you must be clear about who your customers are, what they want, why they want it, and how much they want to pay for it. Whether you're selling a product or a service, standards are set by customers. You have to step into their shoes.

For example, if you're setting up a home daycare business, ask yourself, "Why would someone choose my home?" Are you a nonsmoker? Does your lawn have a fence? Do you have fire alarms and fire extinguishers? Do you serve nutritious meals? Do you stay open later? When you focus on the customer's needs, you'll get their business over and over again, no matter what you sell.

If you're selling products instead of services, you'll find that packaging, the appearance of the product, the price, how the product reaches a customer's home, and how quickly it gets there all determine whether a customer will buy and whether she will buy again.

Internet demographic data for certain locations is available either free or for a small fee. This might include spending trends, the age of people in the area, or the relative income level in the area. Your city's Chamber of Commerce will provide some of this information, and many real estate agents have done this research for you. Demographics can be a powerful tool. Consider what a waste it would be to offer daycare in a part of town dominated by senior citizens.

Do I have a niche market?

The dictionary defines a niche market as a narrowly targeted market, or a special area of demand for a product or service. The trick to finding your niche market is to identify what makes your product or service different from that of your competitors. Then find a group of people with certain characteristics that will make them want your product instead of the others. For instance, you might discover a niche market for childcare services for parents who work at night. If your service offers nighttime support, you will have positioned yourself to be in high demand in that niche market.

You'll put forth a lot of research effort and resources to target people who will be most interested in your ideas and services and to find ways to attract them to your company. Once your business is known as the solution to that narrow market's problem, you may not have to work hard to get business.

What about setting prices and learning how to make a profit?

You will need a price list, unless you're part of a franchise or multilevel marketing company that sets prices for you. The price of your product or service is a key determiner of the amount of your revenue. You must strike a balance between competitive prices and prices that will make a profit. Consumers may also perceive overly cheap prices as an indicator of inferior products or services. Research similar companies and stay in the same price range as your competitors, but try to gain an edge.

Next think about the cost of materials and the amount of time (labor) required for each item or service. You'll also need to consider your overhead costs—business operation costs unrelated to the cost of each individual product or service. These include, for example, rent, utilities, office supplies, and insurance fees. Only a money-making business can pay these expenses, and money only comes in through the price of your products or services. Add up the total overhead costs for a month and then divide it by the number of products or services you'll try to sell in a month. Add that portion of overhead costs to the price of your item. If the overhead costs make your price too high, think about ways to sell more products each month, reduce your overhead expenses, or reduce the cost of your material or labor. Finally, decide how much profit you want to make on each product or service, and add that figure to the price. Setting a price is simply a math problem to be solved.

As you operate your business, ask for feedback. Find out what people think. Customer surveys are one way to learn about your strengths and weaknesses, including problems with your prices. If your products or services aren't selling as you'd hoped, you can advertise a sale. Sale-priced items usually get noticed.

Where will I sell my product?

Depending upon your product, you can sell it from your home, from another person's home, from another retailer's store, or over the Internet. You should develop several different selling options. For instance, perhaps you're selling greeting cards on the Internet using an auction site or your own site. Consider taking a batch to the local craft store and selling on consignment or selling outright at a reduced price. Multiple streams of income using multiple venues to market your product and services will help to build your business faster.

Consider the following:

- Set up a booth at local craft fairs.
- Attend holiday parties where other retailers are marketing their products.
- Think about having "home parties" where you teach others to do what you do, and where they can also purchase your products at the same time (as with Pampered Chef, Arbonne, or Avon).

- Arrange with local craft stores or retailers to sell your products on consignment.
- Place ads in the local newspaper.
- Arrange to place links to your website on other large websites so more people will find their way to your products.
- Arrange to sell through other retailers' websites. Amazon does this for the book market.

What is the best way to keep track of everything I sell?

To keep your business organized and successful, you need to keep written records of the prices you charge, your inventory of products and supplies, and what you sell.

- A well-organized *price list* for all of your products and services will ensure that you're charging the right amount for each item. Make sure everyone in your business has a copy.
- Your *inventory* should list everything you purchase for your business, cost of each item, how much you have of each item, and when you bought it. This helps you know when to restock and how much to buy.
- On a separate list, record *what you sell* and when you sell it. This will help you figure out which items are more popular at different times of the year, and you'll more effectively anticipate sales in the future.

Don't forget to shop around for the best deals on business supplies, and check back with some companies to see if they've lowered prices.

How do I find and pay for a building for my business?

Some businesses require a building or office frontage so your customers can easily find you or for other purposes, like storage. The type of space you'll need and its location also depend on the type of business. A car business requires a high traffic area. A craft store should have big windows out front. If your business supplies services such as on-line graphics, or sells products strictly on-line, you don't need a high-profile space, but you may need the space nonetheless. In a perfect world, that space should be within five or ten minutes of your home. An office that you have no problem "running over to" will help you balance family, personal, and professional time.

Most business owners start selling their product or service from their home and then move to a storefront location when the business grows. If you can't start from home, you should consider renting a building for your first year instead of buying one. The first year of business is critical, and you want to focus more on marketing, making the sale, and building your business, instead of making building repairs, finding the money for down payments, or paying closing costs. Renting also allows you the freedom to move quickly if you find a better location.

If your business needs a larger space, and you're having trouble finding a space to rent, buying is the next best option. Women may get special funding consideration for grants and loans when starting businesses in industries where women are not generally found. Speak to your bank or local small business administration to talk about alternatives for your business funding and purchasing needs.

Finally (and foremost), pray about your business location. Yes, I'm serious. In the field of real estate, I've felt God's presence in my search for locations, including His peace when I've found a spot that works. Put all of your business needs before the Lord, because He cares about every detail of your life.

What's the best way to market my business, to get the word out?

The best way to build a business is to build a reputation of integrity. But marketing and advertising get the word out that you're in business and ready to give people what they need or want. Basic marketing strategies involve telephone books, newspapers, fliers, and word-of-mouth. Almost everyone has a phone book, and that's where people turn when looking for something they need. As you grow, consider the media. You can also advertise in newspapers, but make sure you come up with a catchy or interesting ad to grab the public's attention. I always suggest that people try to generate free publicity by telling their story on local television news stations. If your business or product solves a problem or addresses a controversial issue or current event, pitch it to reporters for all the free publicity you can get. As a news reporter, I saw businesses built on this strategy alone.

To make any kind of advertising work, you must diligently chart the profit and loss ratios for every product line you sell. You need to know which products are most profitable, which you can afford to advertise more, and which to advertise less.

Never forget that the best way to get your name out is by word of mouth. If you do a great job at something, people usually tell others about you. These types of referrals will become the backbone of your business. Each of your customers can be an asset or a liability, so do your best every time. You should also try to stay in contact with past customers to remind them that you're still eager to serve them or their friends.

What do you think of creating fliers for your business?

It's not my favorite choice for advertising, but the pizza restaurant owner we order from regularly would probably disagree. After all, we found him through a flier on our doorknob. Fliers can include general information about your business, or they can sport coupons or special promotions. Your fliers should be informative and nicely designed, with information like prices, your hours of operation, contact phone numbers, and a description of your products or services. If you want to mail or otherwise distribute your fliers, you can contact many agencies in your area for a list of potential clients, or you can use the phone directory.

How important are business cards?

Sounds basic, but it's the first thing potential customers will ask for. Today it's also pretty easy and inexpensive to create a professional business card to help build your reputation and public awareness of your business. Each professional in your company should have his or her own business card with a similar look and feel. Many on-line companies promote this service. Or you can do it yourself or find a local company to handle your designs.

You may also create a logo or short catch-phrase for use on your business cards. The logo might be a picture, a complex graphic, or a simple symbol that represents your company. The catch-phrase can be as easy as "We provide services fast," or "The Art of Giving." Use your logo and catch-phrase also on uniforms and letterhead. In fact, put them on anything you use to communicate with customers and clients, including your website, e-mails, and marketing materials.

How can I find information on effective Internet advertising?

Consider free community bulletin boards and services like Craig's List. Also, if you're really Net savvy, you can search for blogs on topics of interest to your target market. For paid advertising, Google AdWords and Yahoo Search Marketing are two of the most common on-line advertising services. However, both have become much more expensive in recent years, and the bids required to have your name at the top of a search list can be costly. Popular auction sites like eBay can be cost-effective. While you'll make less money per sale because you'll need to price products more competitively, your advertising cost per product is low.

Where can I find great office furniture on a budget?

If you need an office, you'll need some type of furniture for it. With a little time and imagination, you can find what you need even on a tight budget. You don't have to get everything at once; you can add new items as your budget allows. Some sources are bargain outlet stores, garage sales, thrift stores, flea markets, and going-out-of-business sales. Many sellers will negotiate prices, especially on scratched items. And it's not hard to find furniture that is almost new or in great shape. Regular office supply stores offer clearance items or returned items at a discount. Also, at www.freecycle.org you can enter your address and locate office equipment, machinery, furniture and other items being offered for free.

Do I need a computer for my business?

My humble opinion…yes! Why, you ask, if you're operating, say, a landscaping company? Computers make it much easier to stay organized and ahead of the game. With a computer you can easily track and update your files; organize your client information, supplies, and products; generate and print sales and profit reports; and quickly and easily communicate with customers by e-mail (they'll love that).

Software exists for almost every business task—to help you manage payroll, taxes, and expenses; to design your own advertising materials; to scan and store documents (saving file space); to find valuable Internet information to stay prepared for the future; and to sell your products on-line. And more!

A laptop or Tablet PC provides portability and sometimes even wireless Internet access from a variety of locations. You'll have access to important business files wherever you go.

Budget conscious? Would you believe you can actually find working computers at thrift stores?

Do I need Internet services for my business?

In today's marketplace…absolutely! The Internet saves you time, lets you shop and communicate from home, gives you access to resources for building and advertising your business, and allows you to do your banking on-line (double-check your bank's security policy).

Not all information on the Internet can be trusted, but tons of sites provide free ideas, learning resources, tips on advertising, and inexpensive website-building tools or support. Some sites send you free newsletters about how to build your business or free marketing reports. Also, e-mail can be a powerful tool for communicating with customers and other businesses.

Your first step is getting an Internet Service Provider (ISP), which connects you to the Internet for a (usually) moderate monthly fee. Look for ISPs that serve your location. Their packages usually provide e-mail service as well. Once you're hooked up, you'll be on your way to lightning-fast business operations.

Do I really need a website?

A website is a good idea for any kind of business. It reaches into homes and businesses around the world, any time of night or day, to advertise your company. And it allows people to order products or services while you're off playing with your kids!

Believe it or not, you can design your own website. Many bookstores have easy-to-read guides, and it doesn't take long. Your first step is to go to a resource like www.namesecure.com and buy a website address, also known as a Uniform Resource Locator (URL) or domain name. Your domain name will be something like www.thinkthoughtful.com. Buying and registering a domain name isn't terribly costly.

Your Internet Service Provider may offer space for your website. If not, you'll need to find a hosting company that stores your website files for a small monthly or yearly fee. Either way, advertising on the web is a small investment for what might be a big return.

You can pay someone to design your website. But before paying a professional top dollar, consider hiring a local high schooler. Many teens can build a modern looking site for a fraction of the cost of a professional.

What records should I keep?

All businesses deal with a lot of paper and information. As part of your carefully organized filing system, you'll probably make up a file for each customer, containing all pertinent information. Keep this file easily accessible until you're certain you won't need it. Then you can store it away in an attic or storage unit. Before permanently getting rid of the information, consider storing it on a computer or a computer disk. This will come in handy if you ever need to dig up that job or customer again. Protect your clients' confidentiality by keeping all information locked up or otherwise secure.

It's crucial to keep accounting and tax records, including such information as your yearly income, yearly expenses, and records of taxes paid and withheld for your employees. Hopefully you're tracking these financial records with a computer and accounting software. Keep backup copies of those files on a CD or DVD, and label the discs with the year, type of information, and the date of the backup. Store a spare copy in a separate location in case of fire or theft.

Employees or subcontractors—what's the difference?

When you need help with your business, you have two options: employees or subcontractors, each with benefits and drawbacks. For employees, you'll likely pay benefits and additional taxes on their wages. But a trustworthy employee often becomes a great asset to the company, committing to a long-term relationship, increasing sales, and offering ideas for the growth of your business.

You might hire subcontractors to advertise, to perform some step of production, to clean, to perform services, or to store or ship your products. You won't have to worry about workman's compensation or taxes, but subcontractors may cost a bit more, and you might not have a long-term relationship with them. Give them only necessary information, to guard against their taking away your customers or stealing your ideas.

How do you find good employees?

If you find that you're running short on time every day, this is the time to consider hiring an employee to avoid overworking yourself. But searching for good employees isn't easy.

The most basic and inexpensive method is an ad in the local newspaper. In your ad, be specific! If you want someone to type, make typing ability a requirement. If good phone skills are a must, say so. Specify the number of hours per day or week they will work, and mention your business location. Then only people who fit your requirements and can travel to your location will apply, and you won't waste interview time.

You can also place your ad on-line with one of the many local companies offering this service, either free of charge or for a small fee. These companies will sift through the responses and find the best matches. If you're having trouble finding the right candidate, then consider contacting an employment agency. This might cost more, but it can save time and money that you might otherwise spend on the wrong employees.

How do I interview and hire employees?

The company's backbone is the employees and how well they do their job. Finding the right person can be difficult, but be patient and pray. Even

Donald Trump in his book, *How to Get Rich*, says he asks God when it's time to get a new assistant. No joke!

Before an interview, write down the questions you want to ask, including possibly the following. (Other questions will depend on what you feel is important and the type of business.)

- What are your background experiences (such as education and previous jobs)?
- Why do you think you're right for the job?
- What skills will you bring to this business?
- What can you do for this company?
- What are your strengths and weaknesses?
- When are you available to work?
- Do you have reliable transportation to get to work?
- Do you have a criminal record? (Tell them you'll be running a background check.)

Take note of your first impressions. What's your gut feeling about this person? A neat, professional appearance is important; you don't want to hire anyone who doesn't care enough to look nice for the interview. Remember, you will have to work with this person every day. Will this person—one of the faces of your business—work well with your customers?

Ask the candidate to fill out the necessary paperwork for you to do a criminal background check. This is *so* important, for your safety and for the growth of your business. Also contact the candidate's references and past employers.

Should I hire family members or friends?
Some business professionals say this is a bad idea; others think it's the best choice. Here are a few things to keep in mind.

Hiring family members can be to your advantage. Usually they willingly work longer hours or odd hours without overtime pay. They may be more dependable workers because of your relationship. And you can usually trust family members more than relative strangers.

There can also be disadvantages. It may be hard to discipline or correct your family and friends, and if things go sour with that person, it can strain the relationship outside of work. Giving orders can be uncomfortable, especially when they don't follow them.

Ultimately, the decision depends upon the individuals, the nature of the relationships, and the type of business. Think carefully, and talk these issues over with the potential employee before making any final decisions. Decide together what's best, and tell them that if they're hired, they'll be treated like any other employee.

What if I have to fire an employee?

Firing people is hard, but keeping any employee who isn't doing his or her job may be harder—costing you money, valuable time, and possibly the reputation of your business. Communicate often with your employees—perhaps in twice-per-year reviews—to make sure they're doing their jobs and doing them well. It also allows for communication the other direction, helping you understand your employees and seeing whether they're happy. If something needs to change, talk to the employee right away, and make sure that the situation is corrected as soon as possible. Record all reviews in writing.

When an employee isn't doing her job, have a one-on-one talk. It's important never to yell at or lecture an employee in front of another employee. Take her aside and find out what's going on and what you can do together to rectify the situation.

If you've given this employee a chance to improve her actions to no avail, then it may be time to let her go. Try to do this with as much dignity and kindness as possible. Tell her exactly why you're letting her go, what she did wrong, and what you expect of her as she leaves. Tell her when she'll get her last paycheck, and be sure to record all pertinent details in writing.

This is also where your team of experts comes into play. A business attorney will help you handle everything legally.

Do I need liability insurance?

Yes! Any type of business must have liability insurance to protect its profits if something goes wrong. These days it seems that everyone's ready to sue at the drop of a hat. It takes only one buyer to bankrupt you for selling something that caused them bodily injury. Some cases can take months or years to resolve. Liability insurance will cover the bill and help you to bring an end to the case. Chances are you're never going to need it, but the one time you do, it's well worth the cost!

Premiums usually depend on the number of employees. They might also increase if you've made any open claims within a certain amount of time. But insurance can be cheap for many types of businesses. For example, for a typing service, $1,000,000 coverage might be $300 a year. Insurance companies will check your background and quote a premium. Compare different companies for the best price, and ask each company for the names of a few of their customers, so you can ask whether they're satisfied with the service.

Do I need to set regular business hours?

Regular business hours let the public know when they can depend on you and your services. Your customers will appreciate being able to reach you when they expect to. It's good to have your hours printed on your door and included in newspaper, radio, and TV ads.

Having established hours also helps you separate your business time from your home time, which is especially difficult if you have a home office. We all feel that the more work we do, the more successful we'll be, but it's just as important to take breaks. The Bible recommends that we take one day a week off so we can come back to work with more focus and energy.

Regular hours are also important to your employees, as they facilitate scheduling appointments and receiving deliveries. Overall, you'll feel more in control of your business, instead of feeling like your business controls you.

How do I deal with angry customers?

At some point in your business, a customer will complain. Listen patiently and try to understand his point of view. A gentle answer turns away wrath. Remember that your customers are the key to your company's success, and do whatever it takes to make the situation right, within reason. Apologize, make amends if at all possible, or try to find a compromise if the customer's demands are unreasonable. If you end up with a happy customer who retains (or increases) his respect for you, then you've probably gained his long-term loyalty and his word-of-mouth commendation of your business to others. One successful business owner I interviewed says he's learned to see every problem with a customer as an opportunity to endear his business to them.

If you can't resolve the situation in a reasonable way, you may have to end the professional relationship. It's sad, and a little scary, to end a business relationship, but sometimes it's the only way. You'll be better off in the long run without a customer that continuously causes your business hardship and stress.

How can I make my business accessible to everyone?

Both business wisdom and federal and local law dictate that any location other than a home office should be accessible to all employees, potential customers, and business associates. Be careful not to discriminate according to age, race, weight, or ability. Call your local city office and ask for the public accessibility codes in your area, especially as they relate to handicap access. Think about entrances, as well as other passageways and facilities inside your building.

Chapter Six

Protecting Your Ideas

*Discretion will protect you,
and understanding will guard you.*
Proverbs 2:11, niv

Intellectual property matters to more than just a few inventors, artists, and lawyers. If you're in a business that involves authoring, selling, marketing, or coming up with bright ideas, you need to know how to protect your creations from theft or misuse. You also need to understand others' rights to their intellectual property, or you might find yourself on the wrong end of a lawsuit.

The information in this chapter isn't intended to make an intellectual property lawyer of you. But it should give you a working understanding of intellectual property and its protection, enabling you to make educated decisions. For questions beyond the scope of this book, consult the attorney on your team who specializes in this area.

Your intellectual property may become your single most valuable possession.

What is intellectual property?

Property is something you own, plain and simple. You buy a house, it's your property. Along with owning that property come certain rights and the need to protect them. Since the word "intellectual" means "having to do with rational and creative mental ability," the term "intellectual property" refers to the ownership of ideas, creations, inventions, works of art, and so on. Intellectual property is just as much property as is your house. It can be bought and sold, protected, insured, used as collateral, bequeathed, stolen, and, through neglect, wasted or abandoned.

If you were to come up with a clever device that peels oranges automatically, that could be worth a lot of money. Now the idea by itself can't be owned or protected. If you casually mentioned it to a friend and he went off and built the machine and sold it, you wouldn't have a legal leg to stand on. Your idea, to be "intellectual property" in the eyes of the law, must exist in some tangible form. With the orange peeler, you would need to draw up plans, or at least scribble a diagram on the back of a napkin. At that point you have legally turned the idea into intellectual property. You could then take steps to protect that property from unauthorized production or development by others.

If someone writes a poem, he owns it. A photographer who takes a picture owns the reproduction rights to that picture. The same is true for a song, a play, a new device, a new method of doing something, the name of a product, an e-book, a logo, or a software program. All these things qualify as intellectual property, and their ownership can be protected by law. They can also be stolen or infringed upon, and legal action can be taken to prevent this or to restore the property to its rightful owner.

So what happens if I do nothing to protect my intellectual property?

Failure to protect your intellectual property can result in great losses for you. Imagine if Apple hadn't bothered to apply for patents for the iPod. Or, on the other side of the coin, did you know that the graphical user interface (GUI) that became the first Apple Operating System, and later became Microsoft Windows, was developed for internal use by Xerox Corporation at its research and development facility? The company didn't realize the market value of the system its employees developed to communicate with each other. Since Xerox took no steps to register its rights in the software, two smart young men (one of whom is now running Apple) set up shop in a garage and produced the first Apple computers using that same graphical user interface. That painful intellectual property lesson cost Xerox billions of dollars.

So how do you protect your intellectual property?

Three basic methods exist to ensure that you retain full authority to sell, license, deny, or dispose of the rights to your intellectual property. These methods are *patents, copyrights,* and *trademarks.* A fourth method involves *trade secrets*, which usually relate to confidential information within a business (for example, the formula for Coke) and aren't protected the same way. Each type of protection works a little differently, and this chapter will help you understand which means of protection applies to your property.

What is a patent, and under what circumstances should you apply for one?

Basically a patent is a means of protecting an invention, a new and non-obvious way of doing something, an improvement to an existing design or method, or some similar creation. The related documents are called "letters patent." The purpose behind the patent registration process is to give inventors the incentive to publish their great ideas, so that others might start using them as soon as possible. Anyone can then read these documents (the word "patent" means "open to public view"), but they cannot legally infringe on your property rights.

A patent doesn't necessarily give the patent holder all of the rights needed to manufacture the invention or idea. Back to our iPod example. Let's say you came up with a way of making an iPod work as a mobile phone. In order to produce and sell your blended product, you would need the right to manufacture and market the iPod, which you don't have. So if you successfully patent your device, it would only prevent another company or individual from using or producing it. In order to use or develop your idea, you would have to buy a license from Apple, or you could sell a license to Apple to use your invention.

There are three basic types of patents:

Utility Patents are what most of us think of as patents. They deal with function—inventions, ways of doing something, chemical compositions, processes, and so on. Utility patents can be obtained for a thing, a method for making a thing, or a method for using a thing.

Design Patents cover the appearance and aesthetics of something, rather than the function. If you designed an MP3 player in the shape of a space ship with certain specific lines and markings, you could patent that design.

The third type is a *Plant Patent*, which is specialized and of interest only to plant breeders.

Patents remain valid for different periods of time and may have associated fees. Utility patents are issued for a period of twenty years and require a maintenance fee. If you don't pay the fee, your patent is voided. Design patents are valid for fourteen years and do not require a fee to maintain.

Once a patent has expired, the device, technology, method, or process is up for grabs. Patents are national in scope and do not cover use or abuse in other countries, unless you register overseas as well. Patents can't be renewed. Once a patent expires, the idea falls into the public domain and anyone can use it without permission or paying royalties.

What is a copyright, and what does it cover?

A copyright is protection against unauthorized reproduction of some form of expression, such as writing, music, film, a TV show, a work of art, architecture, a musical or theatrical performance, computer software, a photograph, and the like. As soon as someone puts an idea into tangible form (writes the poem or the article, designs the building, paints the painting, or performs the rap piece) she owns the copyright. The copyright belongs to the author. With "works made for hire," the person hiring the actual creator is considered to be the author unless their agreement specifies otherwise.

A copyright restricts people from copying, performing, distributing, or selling your work without your permission. It also dictates that no one can make a new work based on your work. However, note that ideas by themselves are not covered by copyright—only the form of expression. For instance, if someone writes a book containing all the same ideas you expressed in your book, but in different words, they aren't infringing on your copyright.

You aren't required to put a copyright notice on something in order to own the copyright. Nor are you required to register it. You own the copyright in any case, because you're the author. (So if you're thinking of copying someone's work because you see no copyright notice, don't.) However, for the best legal protection and to take action against infringement, you should use copyright notices (© 2006, Your Name) and register the item.

What is a trademark or service mark?

A *trademark* is a protection against unauthorized use of the name or symbol that represents the source of a product. *Service marks* are a subcategory of trademarks, and they protect the name or logo used for a service, rather than a tangible item ("FedEx," for example, is the mark of a service, not a product).

Trademarks can extend to the shape of the packaging or appearance of a product as well (such as a Coke bottle), or even to a certain arrangement of notes (the brief song when Windows opens on your computer). Website domain names fall under trademarks, and you can protect other unique factors of a product or item with a trademark. A trademark can also refer to a slogan, such as Nike's "Just Do It," or any of a thousand other registered slogans that are uniquely associated with a product or service. If Reebok started putting "Just Do It" on their sneakers, there would be trouble.

How do I choose between a patent, a copyright, or a trademark?

Much of this is review, but let me bring it all together here for comparison. If you've invented a device, a substance, a way of doing something (including business methods), an improvement on an existing device, or way of doing something that's useful, non-obvious and novel, you should apply for a utility patent.

If, instead, you've come up with a design or look for something that you want to protect (as opposed to its function), you should apply for a design patent, *and* a trademark in some situations where the shape or design is an important symbol representing the product.

If you've produced a work of art, a book, computer software, poems, photographs, music, plays, performances, or other such expressions, you automatically own the copyright; other people can't legally copy what you've done. But you'll need to register your copyright before you can take steps to enforce your rights against an infringer. (Note that software could be subject to a patent as well as, or instead of, a copyright. But in order to claim a patent, it must fulfill some new and useful function. It's a complicated area. If you've invented a software program and want to protect it, consult with an intellectual property attorney.)

If you want to protect the company name, brand name, or identifying mark that represents the source of your product or service, you should apply for a trademark or a service mark and get it registered at the state and federal level.

Who or what is an "author"? What is "work for hire"?

The person who originally creates a copyrightable work is the author, and he owns the copyright automatically. If more than one person worked together on the project, the copyright is shared by all collaborators.

The only exception is "work done for hire" or "work for hire." If an employee creates something for an employer as a normal part of his employment, unless specified otherwise, the employer is considered the author. So if a writer is employed by a textbook company, the copyright for his textbook writing belongs to the company unless the parties specifically agree to something else in writing.

However, this rule doesn't automatically apply for work done by a consultant, a freelance worker, or an independent contractor. In this case, if the person hiring wants to own the copyright, she needs to have the author (in this case the freelancer) sign a work-for-hire agreement that clearly transfers the copyright to the company or person doing the hiring. If there's no such signed agreement, the copyright is retained by the writer, photographer, composer, or programmer. In cases where a copyright will be transferred, consultants or freelancers can often charge a higher fee.

What is "public domain," and how does it affect copyrights?

Copyrights last for a specific period of time. This period depends on a few different factors, but generally lasts at least seventy years. If the author dies, the copyright usually belongs to his or her heirs. Once the period of the copyright has expired, the work falls into the public domain, which means it's no longer copyrighted and can be copied by anyone. Shakespeare's plays are all in the public domain, so new movie versions of *Romeo and Juliet* can be made freely without permission. If you want a copyright to remain valid for longer than seventy years, seek advice from a specialist in copyright law.

What is copyright infringement?

A copyright is infringed upon when someone has actually copied the work in some manner, sold or displayed the work as his or her own, or produced a derivative work.

The fact that someone else's work is similar or has the same content does not constitute an infringement of copyright if it isn't copied directly. Someone could read a section of this book and state the exact same ideas in a different way, and they wouldn't be doing anything illegal. Remember, it's not the ideas that bear the copyright; it's the form of expression of those ideas—the words of the poem, the actual code of the software program, the photograph or painting itself.

There's a small loophole in copyright restrictions called the "doctrine of fair use" (which sometimes becomes "unfair abuse"). For all other situations, the copyright owner can take legal action to enforce the copyright. According to intellectual property attorney Marshall Martin, if the copyright for the work was registered after first publication or, if unpublished, was registered before the infringement occurred, then the owner can seek statutory damages of up to $150,000 per infringement. Copyright infringement is no laughing matter.

What is a derivative work?

The Copyright Act defines a derivative work as any work based on one or more preexisting works. This includes a translation of a novel, a novel rewritten as a play, a movie made from a novel, an abridged version of a novel, a new rap version of an existing song, and so on. The film *Papillon* is a derivative work of the novel of the same name. Before they could make the movie, the film's producers had to obtain permission from the novel's author. A poster using a Van Gogh painting is also a derivative work, but because Van Gogh's work is in the public domain, his permission is no longer required. That's a good thing because it would certainly be hard to get.

If done with permission, or if the original from which the work is derived is in the public domain, and if the derived work adds considerably to the original, the derived work has its own copyright, which belongs to the person who produced it. However, if a derivative work is done without the permission of the copyright owner and the copyright is still in force, the derivative work becomes an infringement of copyright law.

What is the doctrine of "fair use"?

Be warned that "fair use" has some gray areas, and court rulings have not been very predictable. According to the doctrine of fair use, there are times when you can get away with using material without the approval of the copyright owner or, conversely, someone can use your material without permission and not be liable. If the use can be shown to be in the public interest, as in the case of a newspaper report, a criticism, teaching situations, commentary, or research, you may not succeed in prosecuting the person who copied your work. If the offending person benefits from the use financially, then the copyright owner has a stronger case.

An important factor in decisions about fair use is the proportion of the material used and whether or not the copyright owner is denied legitimate income by the use. If a large portion of the material was copied, or if the copyright owner lost the chance to make money from his or her work, the copying is less likely to be considered fair use.

If in doubt about whether you should use someone else's work or whether you should take action against someone who has used yours, consult an attorney. (The pertinent statute is Title 17 of the United States Code §107.[6])

So what steps should I take to protect my copyright?

As I've said, you technically own the copyright on material that you author the very second you create it, even if you do nothing else. You can still take legal action against an infringer or to prevent further infringement of your copyright. However, practically speaking, in order to make a claim and recover damages from an infringer, you usually must have registered your copyright. So it's worth your time to both register your copyrights and place copyright notices on your work.

It's best to register your work before publication or, for unpublished work, before anyone has a chance to copy it. You need to register each work only once. All you have to do is fill out a form, attach one or two copies of the work plus a small fee (thirty dollars at this writing), and send it to the Library of Congress. When registering software, you do not need to include all of the code, just include part of it. Thankfully, you don't have to give away the whole program in order to register it.

The forms for registering copyrights are available at www.copyright.gov/forms and can be downloaded and printed.

A copyright notice, placed on each of your works, consists of the symbol "©" or the word "Copyright," the year when the work was first published or created, and the name of the copyright owner (for example: "© 1999, Joe Author"). It need appear only once on the work.

Can I use a copyright notice on something for which I haven't registered a copyright?

Absolutely. And you should. If you write an article and send it to an editor for possible publication, put a copyright notice on it. Do the same for photos, music, software, or any other creation. It just might deter some people from unauthorized use. The fact remains that you own the copyright in any case, but you might as well make it clear.

Back to patents. What makes something patentable?

With a utility patent, three key qualities must apply to an invention or other item that can be patented: It must be useful, non-obvious, and novel. *Useful* is easy; it has to do something beneficial. *Novel* means it doesn't already exist. *Non-obvious*, however, is the tricky part. To meet this requirement, someone else of ordinary skill in the related field who tried to solve the same problem wouldn't be likely to come up with your answer. As the patent applicant, you are obligated to disclose to the Patent Office any designs or items already in existence that would have bearing on the determination of whether your item is novel or non-obvious.

What is patent infringement?

The owner of a patent is entitled by law to prevent someone from making, using, offering for sale, selling, or importing into the country the invention that has been patented. In some cases, a patent also applies with regard to an equivalent (but different) device that performs the same function in the same way to accomplish a similar result. If someone breaks one of these rules with an item or design that you've patented, that person has infringed on your patent, and you can take legal action.

A U.S. patent doesn't generally protect your item in other countries, but you can obtain a patent that includes other countries. In most countries patents are awarded on a first-come-first-served basis. If someone in France or Russia applies for a patent on your invention and you haven't taken steps to protect it in that country, they can produce and sell it. They cannot, however, export it to the United States if you already have your U.S. patent.

How do I apply for a utility patent?

You can apply for a provisional or a non-provisional utility patent (visit www.uspto.gov). A *provisional* application is less expensive and enables you to protect your invention in the United States for a limited time. It doesn't grant you a patent, but it gives you twelve months from the date of filing to proceed with a non-provisional application. There are advantages and disadvantages to applying for a provisional patent, and each case has to be weighed on its own merits, preferably with professional help.

If you're applying for a full, *non-provisional* patent, you need to prepare several items, including the title of your invention, a detailed description, possibly one or more drawings, and a filing fee. Non-provisional claims also require an oath or declaration, including the fact that any prior relevant work has been disclosed by the applicant.

If your invention is found to be novel, useful, and non-obvious, the patent is issued and published. Every patent is assigned a unique number, and the manufacturer can and should mark the patent with the number on the item.

Before applying for a patent, conduct a patent search for any existing patents covering your invention or items similar to it. If you discover an existing patent, you'll have saved a lot of your time and money. This type of research will also make it easier to state your case for the novelty, usability, and non-obviousness of the invention and help you identify exactly what aspects of the invention can be covered by the patent.[7]

You should strongly consider getting professional help, especially to correctly phrase the claims section of your application, as this section is crucial in any infringement lawsuit.

How do I apply for a design patent?

Design patents are easier and less expensive to obtain. You'll need to fill out a simple application and provide a drawing or other representation of the item. In your drawing, represent your idea with as little detail as necessary. The more basic the depiction, the broader the coverage of your patent. You can also patent just a portion of the overall design. If someone uses this portion, even if the rest of their design is different, they're still guilty of infringement.

How much money is involved?

Listed below are basic fees you'll pay the United States Patent and Trademark Office (USPTO) for different stages of the process, as of this writing. (The figures noted are for small entities, individuals, and nonprofits. Larger companies pay twice these amounts.)

- *Filing fee*: Utility $150, Design $100
- *Examination fee*: Utility $100, Design $65
- *Issue fee*: Utility $700, Design $400
- *Publication fee*: $300 for either Utility or Design.

Utility patents also require maintenance fees to keep them in force after certain time periods (again, fees for larger companies are higher):

- *Maintenance fee*: $450 for 3½ years; $1,150 for 7½ years; $1,900 for 11½ years.

In addition to these expenses, you may have to pay for a patent search, for a professional draftsman to draw your invention, or for an attorney to write your patent application. Fees for these services vary according to the person performing them and the complexity of the patent.

How long do I have to apply for a patent?

In the U.S., from the point when you first offer your invention for sale, you have a year to submit your patent application to the USPTO. In other countries you must have filed your patent application before offering the item or invention for sale.

Do I need to advise anyone that something is patented?

No. But if you don't, you'll have a harder time claiming damages in a legal proceeding against a patent infringer. It's wise to mark your product with the patent numbers from the moment you start selling it. This marking serves as a warning to the would-be infringer, and the damages start accumulating from the point when the infringement began.

When do patents take effect?

A patent starts protecting you from the date it's issued. In some cases, the protection could be considered retroactive, and a court might award royalties for infringement of a patent back to the time when you applied. Items that are marked "Patent Pending" are therefore protected by patent law. However, the patent must actually have been applied for in order to mark an item "Patent Pending," and it's illegal to use those words when no application has been filed.

More on trademarks. What makes a good trademark?

The easiest trademarks to protect are invented or coined words like Xerox or Kodak, or words like Macintosh or Google that aren't obviously related to the product they stand for. Generic descriptions of items or products—like calling a soft drink "Lemon Juice"—make for trademarks that are difficult or impossible to protect. The more distinctive your trademark, the better. Lawyers will work hard to dissuade you from using a mark that's descriptive of your product, because it's harder to protect it.

What is trademark infringement?

Trademark infringement means that someone else is using the same mark as yours, or using a mark similar to yours. When this happens, consumers can easily become confused as to who's the source of the product or service. It could also make them think that there's a connection between you, the owner of the mark, and the infringer. If the use of registered or owned trademarks creates confusion as to the *source* of the product or service, the trademark has been infringed. In legal proceedings it will be important to show that the infringement has caused confusion in the minds of the public.

For example, if you used the domain name www.intel.com for your computer store, consumers may confuse your company with the company that produces the Intel® technology. Once you have a registered trademark, as long as you use it correctly, you have the exclusive right to use it as a brand name for your products.

How do I make sure the trademark I choose isn't already in use?

You'd be amazed at how many trademarks have been registered. The fact that you may not have heard of one doesn't matter. It's safer and far less costly to confirm in advance that your would-be trademark isn't already in use by someone else, than to discover later that you're infringing on someone else's trademark. Conducting a trademark search—a procedure known as trademark clearance—is not very expensive and should be carried out by a legal firm.

Do I have to register a trademark?

You're not required by law to register a trademark. Unregistered marks are called "common law" marks. By simply using your mark, you establish rights of use. Registering a mark without using it doesn't actually give you exclusive rights to the mark. You can use the sign "TM" (sometimes "SM," for a service mark) to show that you consider a mark to be your property, even before it has been registered. The symbol ® is used once a trademark or service mark has been registered, but it shouldn't be used with an unregistered mark.

Registering your mark at the federal level does have advantages. Registered trademarks are published so others will know not to use it. You can also claim incontestable rights to the mark under certain conditions, and you can list your trademark with U.S. Customs to block attempts to import products that infringe on your mark.

Trademarks can be registered either at the state or federal level. Registration at the federal level reserves the use of your mark across the whole country, which will pay off when you expand your activities beyond your own geographical area.

How do I register my trademark?

Registering a trademark involves an application, some minor fees, and a bit of research. Different fees apply for national or international filing. At the state level, requirements differ from state to state. At the federal level you register with the USPTO, and the process is a little more complex.

For federal registration, you need to prove either that you've been using the mark commercially in the U.S., or that you intend to use it commercially. But it won't be registered until you can show that the mark is actually in use commercially.

In addition, you need to show that the mark you're registering is distinctive and not already in use or easily confused with marks already in use. Distinctive marks, like a coined word for example, can usually be registered immediately. If the USPTO questions its distinctiveness, you can register it only after doing one of the following things: 1) Prove that the mark is associated in the public mind with your product or service, or 2) provide evidence that you've been using the mark continuously for five years. The moral of the story? Distinctiveness is the key! It's usually much easier and less expensive to register a trade or service mark with the USPTO than to register a patent.[8]

How long does a trademark last?

In theory, a trademark can be owned indefinitely, but not without action on your part. Trademarks are valid for a ten-year period, but the registration can be renewed over and over as long as the mark is still in use. During the sixth year, if you prove to the USPTO that you're still using the trademark, you can renew it.

If the trademark isn't used correctly, however, it can cease to distinctively identify the source of the product and become the name for the "generic" item itself instead. Famous historical examples are "aspirin," "thermos," and "elevator." In other words, through incorrect use of the mark, aspirin became the name of a pain reliever instead of the company producing the pain reliever, and the trademark was lost. A trademark should be used as an adjective attached to a general term for the product, not as a noun or on its own. For instance write, "use a Thermos[TM]" or "use a Thermos[TM] brand drink container" instead of "use a thermos." Make sure your advertising and promotional materials are correctly using your trademarks.

How do I protect my intellectual property internationally?

There's no such thing as an "international copyright" or an "international patent." You have to follow the law of the foreign country if you want to protect your work abroad. Most foreign countries do provide protection, however, and there are international treaties and conventions, to which the U.S. is party, for this purpose. The U.S. joined the Berne convention, for example, which gives copyright protection for U.S. authors and artists in all member countries of the convention (which includes most European countries), but you must complete a different application. The Universal Copyright Convention (UCC) similarly affords its own level of protection for these kind of works around the world, but the applications differ to obtain such coverage. To claim this protection your work must at least carry a standard copyright notice.

An author who wishes to protect her work with a copyright in a particular country should first research the rules for protection of foreign works in that country. If possible, you should do this before publishing the work anywhere, since protection may depend on conditions being met at the time of first publication.

Patents are somewhat different. If you want to protect your invention in another country, you need to file a patent application in that country, according to that country's rules. In most countries you need to apply for the patent before you start selling the item. There's no one-year grace period as in the U.S.

It's possible to apply for protection in a number of countries simultaneously by filing an international patent application under the Patent Cooperation Treaty.[9] If you think intellectual property is your field of investment, I strongly encourage you to walk this path with an astute attorney who specializes in this area. This is where wise counsel is vitally important.

CHAPTER SEVEN

Is Your Future in Homes?

She considers a field and buys it;
from her earnings she plants a vineyard.
PROVERBS 31:16

Years of experience in this field of investing have taught me one thing—you either love real estate or you hate it. This isn't for the fainthearted and it's certainly no get-rich-quick game. But if you take the time to do your homework, researching properties and markets, I believe real estate is one of the best investments you can make.

If you're already knowledgeable about investing in real estate, just skip around to the questions that interest you. If you're a novice—this chapter is designed for people with little or no prior knowledge of real estate investment—then start at the beginning and work your way through. Then you'll no longer be a novice.

What is real estate?

Real estate, also known as "real property," just means ownership of land or buildings. It's *real* because it exists and you can walk on it or into it, put fences around it, put "For Sale" signs on it, rent it, build on it, and sell it.

You can divide real estate into two general categories: residential and commercial. Residential property consists of houses, apartments, condominiums—buildings where people live. Commercial property consists of buildings where people work—offices, hotels, warehouses, and so on.

Farm land and buildings tend to be a mixture of residential and commercial.

Why real estate?

Real estate is an excellent investment opportunity because if you deal with it skillfully and knowledgeably you can make a good profit. It's *real* estate; you're dealing with large chunks of solid stuff, which tends to maintain and increase in value. I believe real estate is a good investment choice because of what I call the seven laws of real estate:

1. The Law of Supply and Demand—Everyone needs a place to live and work.

2. The Law of Creativity—You can invest for the long term by holding residential or commercial property and renting it, or you can become a short-term investor by fixing up distressed properties and then reselling them. You can work on your own or with partners, corporations, or limited liability companies.

3. The Law of Consideration—Property forces you to use your mind in taking calculated risks and using careful consideration, as did the woman in Proverbs 31.

4. The Law of OPM (Other People's Money)—You can capitalize on property value growth using a small amount of your money and a large amount of someone else's money (borrowed money) to buy real estate.

5. The Law of OPT (Other People's Time)—You can choose an experienced, competent property manager to supervise your property for you.

6. The Law of Passive Income—When that mortgage is paid off, your property will generate income you can live on.

7. The Law of Tax Advantage—Among other tax benefits, you can write off mortgage interest on investment property.

If you're serious about investing in real estate, you need to know your business, just as in any other business or investment. Those who do their homework, are willing to work hard, and as needed hire experienced experts, can turn real estate into a profitable activity.

How would one invest in real estate?

Investing in real estate means buying land or buildings (or buying land on which you then build) and then using your property to make money. There are many ways to do this.

You can buy an office building, hospital, shopping mall, or other commercial property and then lease the space for offices or stores. You manage the building or pay someone to manage it; your profit is the rent minus your expenses. You still own the building and it can appreciate in value while you're making income off the rental. The same applies to houses, apartments, and condominiums (either individual apartments or condominiums or whole blocks of them). It might be one small office in a building, or several skyscrapers downtown.

You might buy a house that is in disrepair, fix it up to improve its value, and then sell it. You can do the work yourself or pay a contractor. To be profitable, the selling price has to be more than what you paid plus what you put into it plus interest on any loan for it.

You can buy a house at a good price, live in it for a few years while its value increases, and sell it for a profit. In this case the selling price would have to be more than what you paid, plus the cost of improvements, plus the rise in the cost of living during the time you owned it. Then you have a profit.

Or you could purchase a land lot in an area that's currently not desirable, hoping that it will become more desirable in a few years and its value will increase. You'll sell at a profit if the sale price is more than you paid, plus any taxes while you owned it plus the rise in the cost of living and any loan interest.

The many variations can look complicated, but the game boils down to a few basic strategies:

- Buy low, wait, then sell high.
- Buy, build, and sell.
- Buy and rent (and maybe sell).
- Buy and improve, then rent or sell.

And you can do all this with…

- land (residential, commercial, or farming).
- buildings (residential or commercial).

Now isn't that simple? Okay, many types of complexities can and do enter in. But look at it this way: These keep you on your toes and prevent boredom.

The whole area of financing your investment (if you don't have the cash for your real estate purchases) is the subject of countless books and websites, often created by professionals who overly complicate the subject in order to make you think you are dependent on them. But don't start out thinking it's too hard for you to understand. It isn't. It's just another subject that can be learned, and you can become an expert. I'll help you cut through the "finance speak" and understand the language and the principles.

When it comes to specialized knowledge, such as the legalities of real estate, that's why you include lawyers and other professionals as part of your team. They'll share their knowledge and experience for a fee.

And what about the technology of construction, repair, and remodeling? Well, you don't have to be an expert at this to invest in property successfully. That work can be hired out. But even then, there's really no mystery to it.

What's the best real estate investment I can make?

There's no single answer that works for everybody. It depends on how much money you want to invest and how much time and work you want to put into it. It also depends on geographical location, and whether you want to make a fast buck or build up a long-term investment (maybe even to benefit your children and grandchildren).

Here are some general guidelines. If you want to make real estate investment a full-time occupation and your principal source of income, you might consider buying old or distressed property to fix up and sell. Or you might buy several properties as rentals and manage them yourself.

If you want to invest in real estate as a sideline to your main source of income, a good way to start is to buy property at wholesale prices (because of foreclosure and repossession) and then rent it for more than the cost of your mortgage, taxes, and other expenses. You make some extra cash every month, and once the mortgage is paid, you have a valuable property that will continue to provide passive income. You can partner with one or two other investors to lower your initial outlay (and share the profits).

If you find yourself with a pile of spare cash on your hands and you want it to keep up with and surpass inflation and the cost of living, you might buy and keep a piece of land for a good price in a location where it's likely to become more valuable. You can build on it or not. If your ancestors had done that back in the early 1600s with a piece of farmland in what is now central Manhattan and it had stayed in the family all this time, imagine how rich you would be today. That's an extreme example, perhaps, but it makes the point.

So before you decide the best type of real estate investment for you, take plenty of time to answer the basic question: How much time and money do I want to put into this? The answer to that question will put you on the right path.

How should I think about financing?

Your finance options will determine largely what kind of property you invest in. So before you start looking for property, work out how you're going to finance it.

Two kinds of money are available: money that's yours and money you borrow. If you don't have enough cash, then you resort to borrowing. This is known as a mortgage or leverage. Mortgaged property is yours only as long as you fulfill your agreement to pay back the borrowed money plus interest on schedule. If you don't, you forfeit the property to the lender.

Underneath the many complications rests one simple principle: If you do your homework and invest wisely, you can make a profit over and above the cost of the mortgage. If you don't, you can lose your entire investment and end up poorer than when you started. Successful borrowing depends on knowing the ins and outs of the game. Later we'll overview the pros and cons of various ways of financing your real estate—enough to avoid the most common pitfalls and to know what questions to ask.

Once you've made these two initial decisions—what type of real estate to invest in and how you'll finance it, you're ready to move on. The next step for all types of real estate is research. Your success will depend upon someone—you or someone you hire—doing this properly.

How do I find and evaluate properties?

This is where having another expert working for you—a realtor or broker—pays off. Sure, you can find properties through your local newspaper or an on-line real estate service, but the broker's job is to stay on top of the market every day. Try to find one who is honest and really wants to help you, rather than just to make a quick buck.

Unless fixing up distressed properties is your passion (I know people who do nothing else), I suggest looking for a low-maintenance, high-appreciation rental property—something that generates less headache than profit. Search in local resort areas, excellent school districts, college locations, popular city walks, and tourist areas.

Once you've located a potential area, research the various rental rates. Determine the price that you can afford, then calculate the monthly mortgage payments, taxes, and any dues on properties in this area (more about this later). Make sure that the going rental rates will more than cover your mortgage and expenses. If you find that the rent is low due to the demographics, you may need to look elsewhere. The best situation is to buy at a low early-entry price (a one- to two-year-old neighborhood), rent it, and watch the property appreciate over a two- to three-year period. Then you can continue to rent, or sell and reinvest the profit.

What are the pros and cons of residential and commercial properties?

Residential properties usually don't cost as much as commercial. They're also generally easy to rent and resell at any point in time, especially if they're well located. Commercial properties involve more legal restrictions and licenses, and they aren't as easy to liquidate if you need to sell. Commercial leases are often harder to get out of than residential leases. On the other hand, you may benefit from longer leases with quality companies.

Laws about eviction vary greatly from state to state, so gather information specific to your state. This is an important point in choosing between commercial and residential rental property.

Can you give me some pros and cons about other kinds of real estate investments?

Here are some examples:

Foreclosures

Pros: This is a common-sense way to get started in real estate investing. If you can buy the property for a wholesale price and then rent it out for more than your mortgage and expenses, you're on your way to building wealth one month at a time.

Cons: Hidden defects may end up costing a lot more than you'll ever recover. But since foreclosures are sold as-is, once you've bought it, you don't have much recourse.

Fixer-Uppers

Pros: For investors with their repair ducks lined up, this can be a good money maker. Negotiate as low a price as possible and determine what it's really going to cost to fix up the property for rent or sale. Mortgage and repairs comprise most of your real bottom line.

Cons: If you want to flip the property (buy and sell quickly), if you can't project a profit of $30,000-50,000, then you may want to pass. Why? An unseen defect can quickly run into tens of thousands of dollars.

Residential Investment

Pros: A house that's in good shape can rent for years without any major expenses, especially if it was taken care of early on.

Cons: Good rental properties require time and patience to find, so you might wait a while for one. You also have to make sure it's in a desirable area for renting or selling, or you might end up paying the mortgage yourself. The key is homework. It isn't hard to learn what comparable properties are renting for.

Are vacation rentals good deals?

Having never handled one, I can only defer to my friends and interviewees who have. With vacation rentals, great selling points are imperative—near the water, mountain views, within walking distance of the ski village, and so on. Vacation rentals, unlike year-round rentals, can be extremely profitable; you can generate in a few months what you would make in half a year or more with a "normal" residence.

The problem I see with vacation rentals is the high cost of maintaining the property (vacationers expect all the bells and whistles) and the high cost of paying property or resort managers. One investor I know says the keys to his success are buying into a resort early, before property prices skyrocket, and doing much of the maintenance himself. Again, this investment boils down to a numbers game: Will your peak and off-season rentals exceed all the costs of owning the property? If the answer is yes, add to that the property's appreciation (growth in value) and tax breaks and you may have a winner.

I frequently hear about timeshares. Are these worthwhile investments?

A timeshare is a property shared by a number of individuals. Each owner can use the property for a certain time during each year. Timeshare owners almost never have any relation to one another whatsoever.

The typical share for one owner is one week per year, although each owner can purchase multiple weeks. An owner's time is limited to a designated week each year, and prices for the same property vary depending on the demand for that period. For instance, a week on Hilton Head Island, South Carolina, in April will cost far more than a week at the same location in the sweltering heat of August.

Timeshares can be sold or passed down to heirs, as with other forms of real estate. Many people view their timeshare, not only as a great vacation alternative, but also as an investment. Should they decide not to use the property themselves, they can rent it to others. The value of many timeshares increases with the passage of years, so long as the destination remains attractive.

Most timeshare agreements allow owners to trade and swap locations. For instance, an owner in the Bahamas could swap his weekly ownership for a similar timeshare in Hawaii. Many major hotel companies, such as Marriott International, manage and sell resort timeshares. And many agencies specialize in timeshare sales, should you decide to sell.

What are the pros and cons of rehabilitating a "distressed" property?

Distressed properties can be a great investment if you know what you're buying. Inspections prior to making an offer are worth every dime; you must know what needs fixing. But even after inspections, a distressed property is an unopened box of unknowns. After opening up the walls and looking at the state of the plumbing and wiring, you may find more repairs are needed than you thought. Remodeling distressed properties can go smoothly, or it can become a never-ending headache. Set a budget and stick to it. List the must-haves and nice-to-haves. Work with a contractor, family member, or friend who can warn you against getting in over your head financially.

Make sure that all the remodeling money you spend adds value to the property, increasing its worth by more than you're spending. Bathrooms and kitchens are key areas for focus.

Should I do the remodeling and repairs myself or subcontract?

I know many people who have remodeled their homes. This is a tricky job to take on. Some work is easier, like painting, decorative tiling, moldings, and curtains. You may want to hire subcontractors for brick work, exterior stucco, landscaping, plumbing, and so on. Many cities have regulations requiring contractors for some aspects, like electrical wiring. And if you want your insurance to pay a claim after a fire, you'd better have used a licensed electrician.

If you use a contractor to manage the entire job and oversee all subcontractors, you *must* be sure he has a legal license and insurance in case anything goes wrong. And you must have a signed contract detailing all work and costs. Any changes must be documented and initialed; reports of conversations from memory will not stand up if you have to take legal action. You can expect general contracting fees to be approximately 10 percent of the total job.

If you want to manage the subcontractors to save the 10 percent, make a list of the work you believe you can do yourself. List separately what you want to contract out. Ask for recommendations from coworkers and neighbors. Request bids from at least two or three contractors for each job, itemizing labor and materials. Don't allow them to lump items together into one total cost estimate. Then compare each bid to the cost in time and materials if you were to do the work. Keep in mind, if the contractor purchases materials, he'll generally add a 15-20 percent markup. Then evaluate whether it's worth your time and materials savings to do part or all of the job yourself.

Completing the various stages of your remodel in the right order can be challenging, as many depend on others being completed first. Make a master timeline, and be sure you schedule subcontractors according to it (or be sure your main contractor understands your schedule).

How do public auctions work?
Public auctions are generally publicized in the newspaper or on-line. These pertain to real estate foreclosure, bankruptcies, liens, and liquidations. Properties are offered for sale by state and federal agencies, banks, and other private organizations. Most, but not all, set a preview time so you can see the items prior to the auction. At the auction you may bid on the item "as-is." Once your bid is accepted, you're expected to pay the required deposit in full either via bank wire, cashiers check, or cash. In many cases buyers establish a preapproved credit line just for auction transactions.

Is it smart to buy a property "as is"?
I have, but I don't recommend it. When a seller offers a home "as is," it's usually not a good sign. You're smart to leave your options open, so you can obtain a full inspection before completing your purchase. If you find problems, you can either decline to buy or negotiate repairs into the purchase price.

If at any point the realtor becomes aware of an issue—either currently or in previous dealings related to that property—she's required by law to disclose the findings in the property's disclosure statements.

How can I determine how much a property is really worth?

This is a job for an appraiser. Usually the lender recommends a real estate appraiser, and you pay him to prepare a written description of the property and make a formal appraisal of its value. He'll evaluate the property and the neighborhood, look up land values from county sources and sales information for nearby properties, and take into account numerous other factors.

What happens during a home or building inspection?

Prior to obtaining a loan, your lender will ask you to get an inspection and appraisal of the proposed property. The inspector will thoroughly check all of the rooms, make note of any upgrades to major systems, and check to see that they're working properly, take pictures to back up the documentation, and check all of the following:

- structure
- exterior
- roof
- electrical
- plumbing
- heating and cooling
- interior
- insulation and ventilation
- square footage (compared against legal filings)

Inspectors should be backed by comprehensive Professional Liability (Errors and Omissions) and General Liability insurance. Also verify that they're members of your state's Real Estate Inspection Association (REIA) or the American Society of Home Inspectors (ASHI). It's a plus if they're also members of the American Institute of Inspectors (AII) for continuing education.

$$$

Okay, we've covered the general guidelines for choosing a property. Now for the next part: how to get the money.

What are the different mortgage options?

The usual way to pay for property is by an initial down payment and a loan that you pay off in monthly installments (a mortgage). By means of the mortgage, the lending institution is making an investment in you and your property and earns its money through interest you pay. This is big business. The mortgage market is quite competitive, providing you with a wide selection of lenders. So remember, you're a valued potential customer, not someone begging for money.

Research and get quotes from at least three lenders. Some loan charges are large and may not come to your attention until late in the loan process, so ask that the quotes include all related costs. Before you apply, become familiar with the Truth in Lending law, which specifies what lenders must disclose.

Your credit rating is a key factor determining how good a deal you'll get on a mortgage, or even whether you'll get a mortgage at all. (See chapter 2 for a detailed discussion of your credit score, the ways it affects your credit worthiness, and how to improve it.)

Mortgage loans are usually based on a thirty-year repayment (amortization) schedule. Fifteen-year repayment options are becoming more popular. On conventional loans, with each installment you're paying that month's interest and part of the principal. In the early years of the mortgage term, most of your payment is interest. As time goes on, a larger portion of your payment goes toward the principal.

If your down payment was less than 20 percent, then your payments also include a mandatory private mortgage insurance premium.

Let's take a look at just a few of the different types of mortgages.

A *fixed rate mortgage* (FRM) is the most familiar. The fixed rate thirty- or fifteen-year mortgage maintains the same interest rate for its entire term, making it a good choice for those who are willing to take a slightly higher rate in exchange for the guarantee that the rate won't change and payments will be predictable. Fixed rate loans can be harder to qualify for since the first payments are quite a bit higher than those associated with adjustable rate loans.

With FRMs, the shorter the term, the lower the interest rate. A thirty-year loan for the same amount as a fifteen-year loan has lower monthly payments (because less of each payment goes toward the principal), but you pay more in total (because of the higher interest). If you plan to hold a property for a long time, you may want to secure the shortest term you can afford, as it will cost you less overall.

An *adjustable rate mortgage* (ARM) sets a lower rate for the first few months or years, then the interest rate (and your payment) can go up. For example, a "3/1 ARM" has a fixed low rate for the first three years, and then adjusts every year based on an index (but in this case, it can't change by more than 1 percent, the second number in the loan description). Common ARMs are 1/1, 3/1, 5/1, 7/1, and 10/1. The advantage of an ARM is that the initial interest rate is usually lower than that of an FRM. If you don't plan to hold the property for long, this may be a great deal. However, as rates rise, your payments could end up costing you an ARM and a LEG! It's a gamble.

Balloon mortgages are usually shorter-term loans (five to seven years), but the payment is determined as though it were a thirty-year loan. They often have a lower interest rate, and can be easier to qualify for than a tra-ditional fixed mortgage. That's the good news. Here's the reality: At the end of payment period you're required to pay off the balance in full (the balloon payment). This usually requires you to refinance, sell your home, or convert the balloon mortgage to a traditional mortgage at the then-current rates. And who knows what those will be?

Similarly, *interest-only loans* only require that you pay the interest each month for a fixed amount of time, paying nothing toward the principal. After that term (usually five to seven years) your payments jump, and you might be forced to refinance. Proceed with caution, but this type of creative financing may be right if you don't plan to stay in the home for more than a few years, or you know your income will jump significantly.

For many first-time home buyers, *100-percent financing* can be a great deal, at least allowing you to get into the house. The buyer obtains a mortgage that requires no down payment, but their monthly payments must include private mortgage insurance premiums to offset the higher frequency of defaults. Also, many of these buyers can't afford the homes they've purchased.

Mortgage brokers seem to come up with new options every year. But the basic principle is exactly the same: You're borrowing money that you'll repay over an agreed period at an agreed rate, and you pay for the use of the lender's money through interest, which usually amounts to quite a lot more than you're borrowing. The more you pay initially and the faster you can afford to pay back the loan, the less it's going to cost you.

How do I go about getting a mortgage?

Mortgage lenders look for investments that carry the least risk and the highest potential recovery for them if the owner defaults. Many people look at a loan as a service from their bank, and it is. But try to remember that it's also the lender's investment in you and your property. You are valuable to the lender.

First research the type of loan you'll need. Know your credit score prior to contacting a lender. Once again, you can get a free copy of your report by visiting www.annualcreditreport.com. Dispute any mistakes on your credit report right away.

Once you know your FICO score, you can then start to identify the right lender for your needs. If you're seeking a loan with the lowest interest rates, you need a score of 700 or more. Generally with scores in the 600s, financers and lenders will increase your interest rate, and they may attempt to add points. One point means you prepay 1 percent of your loan balance. Each point you pay can lower your rate an eighth to a quarter of a percent.

Get quotes from each lender, including rates and all closing costs. Your credit score and the loan amount requested will help the lender determine these figures. Once you've found a company you want to work with, you can seek prequalification for the loan amount you expect to request when you find the right property. This is not final approval, but it will get the paperwork started. To take the next step, consider going through the application process for a pre-approval. This shows the seller you're a qualified buyer with a loan in place. For a buyer, it's like going shopping with a check in your pocket for a pre-determined amount.

Typically, the lender will want to see W-2 forms for the previous three years, to show you have a steady income. You'll also need proof of monthly wages (bank statements or payment stubs) and other personal information that validates your reliability as a borrower. It's helpful if you've been on the same job, or at least the same line of work, for two years.

If the property is in a growing area, they're more likely to favor the investment. So if your credit is mediocre but you've located a property that has appreciated over the past few years and is projected to continue the pattern, they may overlook some of your negative marks.

Many lenders offer "no doc" or "low doc" loans. These require less documentation and no income validation. For borrowers without a steady income—like commissioned sales women—this can be a great option. But prepare to pay a higher interest rate for the greater risk the lender is taking.

How can I get a good interest rate on my mortgage?

Rates are currently rising, but at this writing I still see competitive rates in the market. One of the most important factors in securing a decent loan is having a good FICO score, as I've mentioned. Lenders also consider your employment history and the amount of your down payment (preferably 20 percent).

But putting 20 percent down isn't easy, especially if you're buying your first house. Lenders understand this, and some offer programs with lower down payments, but higher risk for the bank and therefore higher monthly payments for you. I've already mentioned 100-percent financing (zero down). Another possibility is to finance 10 percent of the mortgage through a second lender. This program is called 80-10-10, because your first mortgage is 80 percent, your second mortgage is 10 percent, and the remaining 10 percent is your down payment. Your second mortgage interest rate will be higher than that on your first mortgage. Your lender can discuss other creative financing options with you.

A reputable mortgage broker can help you secure a good interest rate. Mortgage brokers shop different lenders to find you the best deal.

Shop around. Remember, lenders are competing to get your business.

Why is private mortgage insurance (PMI) necessary?

PMI is extra insurance that lenders require from most homebuyers who borrow more than 80 percent of their home's value—that is, buyers who pay less than 20 percent down. The purpose of PMI is to protect a lender against loss if a borrower defaults on a loan, enabling higher-risk borrowers with less cash to become homeowners.

If you've maintained a good payment history, you can cancel PMI once you pay down your mortgage principal to 80 percent of the home's original purchase price. The lender will also want proof that the property hasn't depreciated below its original value.

Okay, I've found my property, I've applied for the loan. Now what?

You've completed the hardest parts; now it's time for the property settlement. This can be handled by attorneys for the home buyer or seller, the lenders, the title insurance companies, and the escrow companies. Choose someone you trust to protect you from fraud and hidden fees. An attorney will help you gather documents required to process the loan. The closing attorney will order the survey, prepare the required documents outlined in the lender's instructions, verify insurance, order the title search and title insurance policies, review deeds and deeds of trust, and coordinate with all parties. Once you're approved, the loan papers are drawn up, and you review and sign at settlement. The actual closing takes place anywhere from two weeks to one month after application.

How does mortgage amortization work?

Your loan account begins on the first day of the month following the loan's closing day. You pay "interim interest" for the period between the closing day and the day your account begins. Then your mortgage amortization schedule kicks in, and your first monthly payment is due on the first day of the next month.

Lenders usually provide a fifteen-day grace period following each month's due date. Therefore, a payment received on the fifteenth is treated exactly in the same way as a payment received on the first. A payment received after the fifteenth, however, is assessed a late charge. The good news is that late payments are generally not reported to credit agencies unless they're at least thirty days past due.

Any amount you pay above your normal monthly payment goes completely toward your principal, reducing your loan balance. This can also radically reduce the amount of time to pay off the loan, because you're saving years—or decades—of interest on that extra amount of paid principal.

"Negative amortization" means that even though you're paying the agreed-upon monthly payment, your remaining balance is increasing instead of decreasing. This can happen when your payment isn't enough to cover even the monthly interest because of a rate increase. The positive side of negative amortization is that it keeps payments under a certain level if an adjustable rate increases. Not a problem if you don't plan to hold the property for long. However, the negative side is that eventually payments may need to increase considerably to allow the now-larger loan to amortize over its remaining life.

What about when interest rates begin to go up? What are the risks I need to watch for to protect my investment?

I just read this morning's paper about another rate increase. As interest rates continue to climb, you should be aware of the ramifications. Especially if you have an ARM! My advice is to run now to refinance into a fixed rate loan. If you do nothing, your monthly payments will skyrocket. Also note that if you plan to sell in the near future, high interest rates can slow the market, resulting in longer sell times for properties. But don't panic. Plan your strategy now. Remember, real estate is a long-term investment, and this field of investing cycles through good and bad markets.

I've heard you talk about a cash flow analysis. How do I use this?

A cash flow analysis allows you to track your cash as it flows in and out of your personal or business bank accounts. This is critical; you need to know exactly your monthly property costs, compared to your monthly income. In order to maintain a "positive cash flow," you need to continually evaluate all costs, including property taxes, insurance, association dues, monthly maintenance fees, management fees, and potential defaulting renters. The positive or negative figure at the bottom of the analysis statement represents the net outcome of your operating, investing, and financing income and expenses. Generate monthly, quarterly, and yearly analysis statements to help manage your investments. This summary information is also useful for tax preparation.

I have shaky credit and I've heard about owner financing. Why would a seller want to "carry my note"?

Sellers will sometimes do this when they don't need immediate cash for another home, but would like to receive payments at a higher interest rate than their money would make if they sold the property and let the money sit in a bank. A formal promissory note stipulates certain requirements you must abide by.

In essence, the owner elects to be your bank. He lends you money at terms that suit his needs. Just as with a bank, if you default, the seller has the right to foreclose on the property. In some extreme cases I've heard of owners taking the payments and then regaining full ownership of the home if one payment was missed. So be careful how the terms of the contract are worded. The property belongs to the seller until you pay off the loan in full—either out of pocket or by refinancing with a bank.

In many cases owner financing is faster, credit checks may not be necessary, the down payment is minimal if not zero, and the red tape and closing costs are reduced. If this is your choice, please seek a lawyer's advice.

What is title insurance and who needs it?

Title insurance is a policy that guarantees that the property title is free from the problems of hidden liens and claims. Public records relating to the property are searched for problems in the title's ownership and history. The one-time fee for title insurance is usually itemized among the lender's closing costs.

Possible title problems include:

- mistakes in examining records
- forgery
- undisclosed heirs
- liens for unpaid taxes
- liens by contractors
- liens by associations
- lawsuits

If you're financing the home, the lender will require the buyer to purchase lender's title insurance which protects the lender and the amount of the loan, which is usually not the full value of the property. The buyer has the option of purchasing an owner's policy which protects her interest. Title insurance insures you as long as you own the property. So if a problem arises later, the insurance will cover at least some legal fees for defense against a claim.

Do you think refinancing is a good idea?

Refinancing can be both good and bad. It depends on the market, interest rates, your credit score, your overall financial health, and the lender's terms. Another important question: What do you plan to do with the money you pull out of your home? If you hope to invest in a business or another income-producing prospect, it may be a great deal. If you plan to fund your luxury trip around the world, visiting five-star hotels, only to come back to a bigger mortgage payment, you may want to think again. Consider these five points:

1. If a lender uses your FICO score to issue a mortgage or refinance for a family home, they must disclose your credit score. (You may want to

obtain your score yourself, to verify the figure they're using. Remember that you're entitled to one free credit report annually.)

2. If your score is low, you may be charged higher interest rates, loan processing fees, or points.

3. Before you refinance or apply for a new mortgage, check your credit report for errors. Dispute any problems in a formal letter.

4. Comments from the lender regarding higher points due to your credit score are a red flag. If you're being pressured to refinance and the lender is moving swiftly, this often means they're trying to slip in additional fees. Be sure to have all fees detailed in writing prior to the loan document stage.

5. Check for a mortgage prepayment penalty. This can be quite steep if you pay extra toward your loan or pay it off early.

What are the liability issues related to owning rental property? Will an umbrella insurance policy cover this?

Do you have any assets that you don't want to put at risk in the event of a lawsuit, accident, or catastrophic event? If you said yes, then you need umbrella insurance!

Umbrella insurance provides added liability protection beyond the limits on homeowner's and other personal insurance policies. It typically covers such eventualities as false claims, libel, slander, and vandalism by minors, which helps me sleep better at night! With an umbrella policy you can add an extra one to five million dollars in liability protection. These policies vary in coverage, so check carefully what you're getting.

There are so many liabilities associated with owning rentals that I highly recommend not only that you carry umbrella insurance, but also that you require the renter to carry renter's insurance. The average cost of renter's insurance is $2,300 per year, covering approximately $30,000-50,000 in property and providing typically $100,000 of liability coverage. Check with local providers for exact rates. Benefits to the renter are replacement or repair of their damaged property in the event of a bad storm, a fire, theft, a water leak, and so on. Uninsured renters who incur such losses will come straight to you for reimbursement, whether they have the right or not.

To protect wealth or assets against potential lawsuits, consider also holding your real estate in a limited liability company or even a land trust. But before transferring title, be sure to check your lender's "due on sale" clause, which protects the lender should you assign your property to someone else, even your own company. It allows them to "call" the loan—that is, demand payment in full. Also, buying real estate through a company could end up costing you higher interest rates. A competent real estate attorney can help you assess your risk level.

What are the pros and cons of managing rental property myself?
In many cases this job seems a lot easier than it really is.

Pros: You save the money that you would otherwise pay to a property manager. Also, you have a hands-on view of the state of your property. If the renters are damaging anything, you can give them notice to repair the damages immediately.

Cons: You'll have to constantly pester late payers. When needed, eviction proceedings can take months and much of your time. And picky renters can be very demanding.

Property managers handle all aspects of the renter application process and take all of the other headaches off your hands. If you have kids, work full time, and are generally run off your feet—hire a manager or a management company.

How much does a property manager charge, and how do I find a good one?

The cost is approximately 10 percent of the total income from tenants, depending on your location, the company, and their services. It's higher in some areas of the country and much higher for resort properties. To locate a property manager, call your local realtor. To confirm her quality, check several references. Larger management companies may be able to find renters when you have openings. Smaller companies may give you more personalized service.

Can you explain some of the tax benefits of real estate investing?

With real estate, taxes work for and against you. While local governments often charge annual property tax, you're entitled to itemize real estate tax (including taxes for second homes) on your federal return. Property taxes are often tacked onto your monthly mortgage payments to the bank, unless you request otherwise. The bank keeps the tax money in an escrow account, then pays your taxes to the proper authority on their due date.

You're allowed to itemize mortgage interest payments as a tax deduction, and you may also have other tax advantages related to property improvements. This is another area in which to seek help from a professional tax adviser, who can help you find deductions you might not know about, and can prevent you from inadvertently breaking any tax laws.

How do tax-free 1031 Exchanges work?

A 1031 Exchange is great way for an investor to sell and trade up to a better property without taking an immediate tax hit. But the rules associated with Section 1.1031 of the Internal Revenue Code are complicated; you'll need a real estate attorney or CPA by your side. Basically, this allows owners of certain types of "like kind" property (land, rental, and business) to sell and buy other property without paying the capital gains tax. The catch is that you, the investor, must keep your hands off the proceeds from the sale. An intermediate party handles the money, which must all go toward another property within a certain time frame.

What are some areas of concern with real estate investing?

The keys to navigating the complexities of real estate investing are great research, knowing your market, and understanding the benefits and potential pitfalls prior to investing.

Areas to be aware of:

1. Inflated pricing on new homes. If you buy high and the properties drop in value, you can end up owing more than the property is worth.

2. Adjustable interest rates (ARMs). These may look enticing at first, but get ready for higher rates and higher payments if you don't select the right terms. A mortgage broker I've worked with suggests that buyers use ARMs only to get into a house, make twelve on-time payments to establish a good credit history, and then refinance after one year to a fixed conventional mortgage to stabilize payments. This works well only if the property appreciates, so be cautious about using ARMs. Another possibility many buyers don't consider is a ten-year, interest-only adjustable rate mortgage. This gives you a fixed rate for ten years

before that higher payment is due, allowing you more time to consider your goals for the property. The downside is uncertainty about interest rates in a decade, should you need to refinance that home.

3. Market timing. Many people put their homes on the market after the New Year, creating a wider selection of properties. That's great news if you're a buyer, but it can hurt you if you're selling your property in a competitive market.

4. Market hype. Anxiety about mortgage rates going up or down can sometimes change the tone of the market. Low rates can pique the interest of buyers, but they can also work in the opposite direction. Warnings about climbing rates can slow the buyers' market, making it hard to sell. A successful investor is aware of market hype or fears and takes a slow, steady, reasoned approach to building wealth for the long term.

5. Desirable zip codes. Location is key to both buyer and seller. Properties in desirable zip codes are harder to find and purchase, because the homes don't go up for sale as often. Houses in this market sector can often be inflated in price. You often see skyrocketing prices with coastal properties, lakefront properties, and village locations. Research the market in your area to decide whether the extra cost is worth the return on your investment.

How can I find a real estate investment group in my area?

It's easier than you think, thanks to the Internet. Go to Google and type in "real estate investment club YOUR CITY" and take your pick. Also check with your local financial and investment advisers.

A CLOSING COMMENT

Real estate. If it's good enough for the Proverbs 31 woman, it's good enough for me. And did you know that the prophet Jeremiah invested in real estate? Seriously. Check out Jeremiah, chapter 32.

But don't forget the most important principles. Understand your market and current trends. Know your overall financial status—your short- and long-term cash flow. Invest wisely with the goal of property appreciation. Don't jump into a mortgage without fully understanding the terms and conditions. Consider hiring a management firm to ease the pain of property management. Buy umbrella insurance to protect your assets.

And by all means make money and have fun doing it!

$$\$\$\$$$

More References:

- http://www.bankrate.com
- http://www.myfico.com
- https://www.kiplinger.com
- http://www.completetax.com
- http://www.nareit.com
- http://www.1031exchangeoptions.com
- http://www.investopedia.com/categories/realestate.asp
- http://www.reitnet.com
- http://www.rebuz.com

- http://www.frbsf.org
- https://www.lendingleaders.com
- http://www.taxes.big.com
- http://www.real-estate-owner.com (This is a super link. It leads to all tax-related areas regarding real estate!)

PART III

Smile at Your Future

CHAPTER EIGHT

Taking Charge of Your Retirement

Strength and dignity are her clothing,
and she smiles at the future.

PROVERBS 31:25

The Proverbs 31 woman didn't fear the future. In fact, another version of this verse says, "She is full of joy about the future" (New Life Version). With a lot of prayer and a little planning, you can also experience joy about your future and that of your family.

If you're like most Americans, you'll spend the majority of your life in the workforce, collecting a regular paycheck. Then retirement arrives. Perhaps you've set aside some money to cushion the blow when the salary stops flowing. Or—as is all too common among Americans—you somehow failed to anticipate this day, and your nest egg is fried. Don't worry. It's never too late to secure a solid future.

When you're just starting out in your career, retirement is so far off that you can't envision it, let alone stash some of your newfound cash to fund it. Before long you're scrimping to save a down payment on a home. Then you're into child care and preschool. You're more concerned with your youngster's college education than financing your golden years. With a mortgage to pay and a family to support, how can you possibly set anything aside?

Years go whizzing past, and suddenly retirement is not just visible on the horizon, but quickly closing in. What are you going to live on?

If you had formulated and followed a retirement plan, the answer would be easy. Through careful—but not terribly complicated—planning, you can make smarter use of your income and fund a comfortable retirement while still paying for all those other life expenses. In this chapter you'll learn how to prepare a retirement plan—how much money you'll need, where to find it, and how to handle your affairs so you can relax and enjoy your retirement years. You've earned it—literally.

What is a retirement plan?

A retirement plan addresses your financial and lifestyle needs for the years after you stop working. Retirement might come well before you're considered a senior citizen, or many years after. Your plan identifies how you want to spend your work-free years and provides for an income once the regular paycheck ends. Do you want to head south and enjoy golfing year round? Does travel sound good to you? Maybe you'd like to move closer to family or get involved in a hobby.

Whatever your vision, your retirement plan creates a means to make your dream a reality. It involves managing investments, many of which will shift in later years toward stability and away from risk. The plan also covers other issues associated with aging, such as acquiring insurance for long-term care and organizing your estate for your heirs. Think of your plan as your blueprint for building a comfortable retirement.

Why do I need one?

A steady income, with occasional increases, gives you a sense of security and the confidence to enhance your lifestyle. When you're living on a fixed income, you don't have the same latitude. When the unexpected occurs—like uninsured medical expenses or the need for a new car—how are you going to pay for it?

In today's America, people are living longer and saving less. And while prior generations got some relief from Social Security, the future of this federal program isn't guaranteed. So you have to take control of your post-work details and establish a strategy for giving yourself the rewards of all those working years.

A retirement plan is proactive rather than reactive. By looking ahead to financial needs, health, housing, and other concerns, you can plan intelligently to transform potential crises into manageable tasks. By incorporating an estate plan into your retirement strategy, you also relieve your loved ones of the stresses of allocating your assets and accommodating your wishes after your death.

When is the best time to make a plan?

Immediately, if not sooner. The earlier you start managing your investments to anticipate retirement, the more comfortable you'll be when you're ready to stop working. You may even be able to retire early and enjoy more years without career pressures.

Can I do it myself, or do I need to hire a professional?

Certainly you can handle portions of your retirement plan on your own, but you should have some help with other areas. For example, your will and trust require legal assistance. Your investment portfolio might benefit from the services of a financial planner or adviser. And an insurance agent can help with coverage for life and long-term care policies. I'll help you with some of the fundamentals of building passive income and asking the right questions, but your investment in hiring these professionals will enhance your returns and peace of mind. You will have prepared your future with the experience of seasoned pros.

Where do I start?

Begin by identifying your retirement goals. Where do you want to live? Will you sell your home and move to a warmer climate, or perhaps a smaller home or condo near your family? How do you want to spend your abundant free time? Visit all those places you never had time to see? Fill up your passport with stamps from around the world? Hop into a Winnebago and see this country close-up? Some retirees dedicate their free time and skills to helping others by volunteering. Others retire from one career only to start another. Picture your ideal vision of retirement before you start making your plan. You've started many a sentence with "When I retire, I'm going to…" Your first step is to fill in the blanks. Make a list. Be specific. Before you can follow your dreams, you need to know the cost of the journey.

How do I estimate my future financial needs?

According to a survey by the Employee Benefit Research Institute (EBRI), about 60 percent of American workers don't even attempt to calculate their financial needs for retirement.[10] Of the remaining 40 percent who tried, 10 percent just guessed. Is that how you want to plan your entire future?

An effective retirement plan isn't based on guesses. More often than not, your guess will be way off, and you won't discover it until it's too late! So instead, let's look at how you can analyze your cash flow needs.

Examine your expenses. Look at fixed expenses like housing and associated costs. Figure in variable expenses like health costs, automobile maintenance, travel, and other occasional expenses. Take a hard look at necessities and trim your costs wherever possible, but keep it realistic, and make adjustments for inflation. Don't underestimate your needs. Unfortunately, the cost of living will rise, but your income may be fixed. Inflation averages about 4 percent per year; use this figure to estimate annual increases. If you have rental properties, the good news is your profits from rents should rise with inflation.

Next, determine the amount of income you'll need to replace your working salary. The income replacement ratio is the percentage of your pre-retirement salary that you'll need to support your lifestyle during retirement. Retirement expenses are usually less, since you aren't commuting to work or spending money on clothing, entertainment—all those lunches out—and other work-related needs. This ratio typically ranges from 72 to 82 percent; the lower number applies to a one-income family making approximately $60,000 a year. Lesser incomes will require a higher income replacement ratio, as they can't afford to sacrifice as much. Let's say you were making $60,000 a year prior to retiring. If you'll need to retain about 72 percent of this, your annual retirement income should be $43,200. This is the absolute minimum. If you hope to travel or plan for unexpected health care needs, plan for a higher percentage.

The age at which you retire should be considered when you calculate your income needs. If you retire at 55 rather than 65 or 70, you'll need to plan an income for the additional retirement years.

Look at your income opportunities. Where will you get your income from to support your projected retirement expenses? Social Security benefits, pension, retirement accounts, capital gains on investments, dividends, business investments, and rental property income are all examples of income sources. If, for example, Social Security will pay you $1000 a month, that's $12,000 a year. Deduct that from the $43,200 in the above example, and you now need to find $31,200 in annual revenue through other income opportunities.

Consider your tax situation. Your retirement plan needs to incorporate your tax liabilities. Perhaps you can adjust your income and expenses to minimize your taxable assets. Take into account the reduced tax rate on your lower retirement income—if it is indeed lower. Look at the taxes you'll pay on retirement account withdrawals, unless you have a Roth IRA, in which case you already paid the taxes. Also be aware of your pre-retirement tax bracket when preparing your plan. Depending on the rate, you might want to make adjustments to your earnings before you retire, in order to lessen the pain of your current income taxes.

Evaluate your net worth. Make a list of your assets, including real estate, investments, retirement accounts, pensions, savings, and other property. (This figure will also help later in this chapter when we look at trusts.) Calculate the taxes you'll pay on retirement account withdrawals and capital gains on investments.

Now subtract your expenses from your income. If you end up with a positive number, you're in good shape, at least for the early years. However, if you have a shortfall, you need to plan now to increase your retirement income or reduce your projected expenses—or both.

Now that you have some grasp of your future financial needs, let's take a look at ways that careful planning can help you achieve this goal.

ABOUT RETIREMENT ACCOUNTS

The Individual Retirement Account (IRA) is a government-sponsored, personal retirement program that offers distinct tax advantages. IRAs have become extremely popular since Congress established them through the Employee Retirement Income Security Act (ERISA) in 1974 to encourage Americans to save tax-deferred income for retirement. Suddenly workers with no investment portfolios were growing a nest egg without straining their budget.

With their growing popularity, the plans have been diversified, offering different benefits for pre- and post-tax dollars and providing for different types of savings goals, including funding a college education. Some plans are specialized for certain occupations, such as clergy, teachers, and government employees. By the end of 2002, American workers had contributed an estimated $2.33 trillion to IRA accounts.[11]

Some of what follows is review from chapter 4. Here I'll focus on aspects directly related to retirement planning. Please refer back to chapter 4 for more information about retirement accounts.

What are my choices?

One retirement plan does not fit all. Each has its own benefits, eligibility requirements, and restrictions. Here are some of the most common plans:

401(k) and 403(b). Both are offered only through an employer for eligible workers. Contributions are not taxed until money is withdrawn. Employers may or may not make contributions in addition to yours. A 403(b) is restricted to employees of public schools, certain tax-exempt organizations, and some members of the clergy.

Traditional IRA. Anyone earning a taxable income can open a Traditional IRA, because it isn't an employer-sponsored retirement plan. Income taxes are deferred on contributions until money is withdrawn.

SEP IRA. The Simplified Employee Pension Plan is an employer-sponsored plan, available even to self-employed individuals and sole proprietorships. Only employers, at their own discretion, can make the tax-deferred contributions on behalf of employees.

SIMPLE IRA. The Savings Incentive Match Plan for Employees is an employer-sponsored program. Employees can contribute pre-tax dollars, and the employer is required to contribute as well.

Roth IRA. Individuals can fund a Roth IRA with contributions that have already been taxed, and as the funds grow, no additional taxes will be deducted if you meet the requirements.

Roth 401(k). New as of January 2006, this hybrid blends the post-tax contributions of a Roth with the employer contributions of a 401(k).

Is it too late to start investing?

It's never too soon or too late to explore investment opportunities. But the sooner you start, the more you'll accumulate before retirement. Early in your career you can take advantage of the higher return on riskier invest-ments, knowing that you have time to make up losses. Once you've hit your forties, you need to more seriously evaluate risk factors and perhaps weight your portfolio more heavily toward a less aggressive strategy.

What is a catch-up provision?

The government has placed limits on annual contributions to various re-tirement accounts. A 401(k), for example, has a cap of $15,000 per year.[12] However, if you're fifty or older, you can contribute $20,000 per year and your Roth contributions can go up to $5,000. In the year 2008, that num-ber goes up to $6,000. This is known as a catch-up provision, allowing late starters to make up for lost time. Catch-up provisions vary for different types of accounts; some offer an annual increase of only $500 to $1,000.

Can I have a 401(k) and another IRA?

Yes, you can maintain numerous retirement accounts, but your total contri-butions are subject to limits, and Roth contributions may be subject to your adjusted gross income. You can, for example, contribute $15,000 to your 401(k) and in the same year deposit $4,000 in a Roth IRA.

What's a rollover?

You can move—or roll over—the funds from one retirement account to another without paying taxes or penalties, unless you take a distribution. When you switch jobs, you might roll over the funds from your original 401(k) to a new 401(k) in which your new employer matches your contributions.

What is a defined benefit plan?

There are two types of pension plans: a defined contribution plan and a defined benefit plan. A defined contribution plan [like the 401(k) and 403(b)] lets you make voluntary contributions to a retirement account. On the other hand, with a defined benefit plan you don't make contributions, but are guaranteed a specified monthly benefit at retirement. These are the pensions many of our parents had in which their companies funded the majority of their retirement. The amount can be a certain dollar amount, but is more often determined by your salary and number of years of service to the company. Great news for the older generation; bad news for many of us younger baby boomers and generation-Xers who won't be offered this type of plan. The game changed with ERISA in 1974, putting the onus on us to take charge of our retirement.

The bottom line: A defined contribution plan offers tax-deferred savings and gives you control over how much money is invested in the plan. The key to success is investing something. On the other hand, a defined benefit plan provides a guaranteed retirement income without any investment from you, but you have no control over how much the payments will be.

What is a cash balance plan?

This is a defined benefit plan with certain characteristics of a defined contribution plan, like a stated account balance. Basically, the employee's account is credited each year with a pay credit from her employer, which may be a certain percent of compensation (5%). She will also get an interest credit that may be a fixed rate or a variable rate linked to an index. When the participant retires, her benefits are defined in terms of her account balance, and she can usually take them in a lump sum or an annuity. If you have questions about your cash balance plan, pay a visit to your human resources department. These members of your financial team should have all the particulars of your plan, and best of all, their services to you are free.

When can I make withdrawals from my retirement account without penalty?

Ordinarily, you must be at least 59 1/2 to take distributions from a retirement account without paying the 10 percent penalty. But there are exceptions. For instance, if you become disabled or can demonstrate financial hardship, the penalty may be waived. Some employers will allow you to borrow funds in your account, essentially giving yourself a loan.

What about minimum withdrawals?

With a Traditional IRA or 401(k) you must take a minimum required distribution (MRD) by April 1 of the year following the year you turn 70 ½, because the government doesn't want to wait forever to collect the taxes. A Roth IRA does not require this, because you've already paid the taxes.

INVESTING FOR THE FUTURE

Smart retirement planning is more than just putting money away; it's letting that money work for you, making more gains. It doesn't take a financial wizard to profit from stocks, bonds, mutual funds, and other securities. You just need to understand your options and the risk and reward of each.

We discussed much of this in chapter 4, so please read it for more information. This section will emphasize investment from a retirement planning perspective.

If you haven't begun investing, talk to a certified financial planner or investment adviser about the best way to get started. Ask your banker for the names of reputable advisers. And look for an investment course, local or on-line.

What is the best choice for investments?

The answer depends on your goals and risk tolerance. If you have an aggressive goal for making money, choose stocks and commodities, which deliver higher returns. This means greater risk, but with wisdom and patience, statistics show that stocks outperform any other investment over the long haul. Mutual funds fall into various categories; some are more cautiously invested than others. Lower-risk, lower-return choices include bonds, CDs, money market accounts, and IRAs.

How diversified should my portfolio be?

Diversifying means not relying on a narrow group of investments. Weighting your portfolio on the high-risk side could prove disastrous if your gamble doesn't pay off. Being too cautious might not give you the growth to sustain you during your retirement years. A well-diversified portfolio incorporates both ends of the risk spectrum.

The younger you are, the more risk you can take, because you have time to rebuild in the event of a nasty hit. As you reach the middle of your career, reduce your vulnerability by steering your portfolio toward more moderate risks—blue chip rather than small cap stocks, for example.

How often should I make adjustments to my portfolio?

You should track your portfolio's activity regularly. If the stock market fluctuates up or down, and your portfolio is heavily weighted toward stocks, you may want to do some trading. Read each mutual fund prospectus that's regularly mailed to you to track fund performance and consider whether you should shift money to a different fund. As you age, you should probably adjust to a lesser degree of risk, to protect against loss that you can't make up before retirement.

What is a variable annuity?

Similar to a retirement account, a variable annuity is a contractual agreement with a life insurance company that repays you a lump sum in the future or provides a regular income stream. You pay premiums that are invested by the insurance company in securities and fixed interest accounts. Your money earns tax-deferred interest. As with an IRA, you incur a 10 percent federal tax penalty for withdrawals before age 59 1/2.

The insurance company maintains an annuities investment portfolio, managed by a professional manager, that's separate from its general investment portfolio. Options include portfolios of stocks, bonds, and money market instruments. You can diversify by buying units in different portfolios.

How do I purchase an annuity?

You pay either one large sum or separate payments to the life insurance company. You're actually buying "accumulation units"—shares in the total worth of the company's annuities investment portfolio. If the portfolio is worth $10 million, for example, and has one million accumulation units, each unit is valued at $10. As the portfolio appreciates, the value of your unit increases.

What does it mean to "annuitize"?

When you annuitize, you opt to receive payments from your annuity at regular intervals rather than in one large payout. You can choose from a variety of options, depending on how you want to spread out the income.

What are the tax consequences of annuities?

If your premiums were paid with post-tax dollars, then when you receive an annuity payment, you pay taxes only on the interest earned. Withdrawals are always taken from accrued interest before touching the principal, so expect to pay income tax when you receive earlier payments.

If you purchased your annuity in a qualified plan, such as an IRA where the investment is pre-tax, you pay taxes on all payments.

Are there any guarantees with annuities?

Annuities carry some risk, but some let you allocate a portion to an investment with a guaranteed fixed interest rate. Also check to see if your annuity has a guaranteed death benefit, which gives your beneficiary either the current contract value of your investments (minus any withdrawals) or the total of your premiums, whichever is greater.

How do annuities compare with other retirement accounts?

Both annuities and IRAs offer tax-deferred growth, but annuities have a few advantages you should consider. For example, you can open an IRA only with earned income, such as salary, wages, bonuses, and commissions. Annuities have no such restriction. In addition, there's no limit to the amount you can invest in an annuity. Some IRAs have income requirements, but annuities do not.

The IRS requires IRA holders to begin taking distributions by age 70 ½. Most annuities allow you to wait until age 85.

Most annuities are similar to a Roth IRA; contributions are post-tax. The advantage comes when you make withdrawals. With a Roth, however, your earnings are tax-free if you meet the requirements, whereas the interest on your annuity will be taxed when withdrawn.

EXAMINE YOUR ESTATE

Benjamin Franklin said, "In this world nothing can be said to be certain, except death and taxes." Franklin's words could be the motto for estate planners, for whom death and taxes are the two biggest realities. How will your assets be handled after your death? If you become incapacitated, who will make decisions on your behalf? If you have specific wishes for your funeral, have you made them clear?

As morbid as it sounds, too many people neglect these issues until it's too late. Avoid creating an undue burden for your loved ones. Taking time to plan your estate will provide peace of mind for you and minimize the unsettling—and potentially contentious—details for your family.

What is an estate plan?

An estate plan provides instructions for handling essential details when you become too ill or after your death. Your plan incorporates a will, the assignment of power of attorney, a living will or health care proxy, provisions for long-term care, and perhaps a trust.

Why do I need one?

Mainly, an estate plan gives you control over your lifelong gains. You determine who will handle distribution of your assets, minimize tax burdens on your heirs, and provide direction for your medical care and funeral. If you've ever heard about family members squabbling over property, or waiting out an extended probate process, or even struggling over caring for a loved one who's critically ill, you can understand the value of an estate plan.

Do I have a large enough estate?

Estate plans are not just for the wealthy. Your home, your car, your personal property, savings, retirement accounts, investments, and insurance policies can add up to more than you imagined. And your estate plan also establishes guidelines for someone to follow your wishes when you can't do it yourself.

How do I start to make a plan?

Take an inventory of your assets. Make a detailed list of your property—including real estate and valuables—investments, retirement accounts, savings, insurance policies, and business interests. Estimate the value for each.

Next, identify whom you want to inherit various assets. Think about whom you can trust to handle your financial matters, and assign that person power of attorney and responsibility as executor of your will. Should the same individual make medical decisions for you? What funeral arrangements do you want? Are the beneficiaries on your accounts and the policies up-to-date? Write all this down, preparing to convert your wishes into legal commands.

Who should handle my estate planning?

Because of the legal issues, talk to a lawyer who specializes in estates. He can prepare legal documents and help you understand estate taxes. In some cases, you can make adjustments to your estate—such as tax-free gifts—to reduce the tax burden.

How much estate tax will my heirs have to pay?

If your estate is worth less than $2 million, nothing. In 2009, the ceiling will rise to $3.5 million. By 2010, Congress is expected to repeal the estate tax altogether. While this sounds like a generous gesture by the U.S. government, understand that nothing is certain with Congress. There's some question as to whether the repeal will become reality.

In the meantime, take into account the compounding value of your retirement accounts, investments, and life insurance benefits. Your estate won't likely grow beyond the tax-free mark. But if it does, your heirs will pay estate tax of almost half of every dollar exceeding the limit. So if you die in 2008 and leave an estate worth $2.2 million, your heirs will pay close to $100,000 in estate taxes! An estate lawyer or tax adviser can help you reduce your estate's value without compromising your lifestyle or the inheritance you leave your heirs.

Is there an advantage to reducing my estate by making gifts?

Absolutely! You can make gifts of up to $12,000 per year to an individual without owing any federal gift tax. This means that, within limits, you can give your children or other heirs part of their inheritance while you're still alive. A gift is defined as any property transferred to someone else at less than its full value. You could give an education gift by paying college expenses for a grandchild, for example, and also give that person up to $12,000 a year without exceeding the limits of gift tax.

Should I discuss my estate plan with my heirs?

Yes. It's a good idea to discuss the details in order to avoid misunderstandings. You can also deal with possible problems and make adjustments. Let these people know your wishes if you become incapacitated, and where the legal documents are kept. An excellent book for handling the emotional side of estate planning is *Creating the Good Will* by Elizabeth Arnold.

Why do I need to include power of attorney?

By choosing and directing an "agent" or "attorney in fact"—the person vested with power of attorney—you retain control over certain decisions should you become incapacitated. A stroke, for example, could leave you unable to handle your financial affairs. Your spouse might be prevented from conducting even the simplest financial dealings—even movement of funds to pay your medical expenses—unless you've assigned power of attorney.

What's the difference between springing and durable power of attorney?

A springing power of attorney takes effect under certain conditions that you establish. It might require a letter from a physician or a court order to specify that you're unable to make your own decisions. A durable power of attorney is effective immediately after you become incapacitated and requires no other documentation.

What happens if I become incapacitated before assigning power of attorney?

Your family will need to petition the court to assign power of attorney. This can be a time-consuming process, and the court-assigned agent might not have been your choice.

Do I compensate someone to act as guardian of my affairs?

When the agent is a family member or friend, you probably won't have to pay a fee. If you appoint a lawyer, banker, or other professional, you'll need to determine compensation. The fee could be an hourly charge or a percentage of the assets being managed.

What is a health care proxy?

A health care proxy is similar to power of attorney, but this individual is limited to managing your medical concerns when you're incapacitated. This is always referred to as "medical power of attorney" or "health care agent." This individual must understand medical information to assess treatment options, be able to make difficult decisions under stress, and know (and respect) your wishes.

WILLS AND TRUSTS

These aren't complicated, but as with any other legal document, you should know what you're getting into before you sign.

What's the difference between a will and a trust?

Both affect how your estate is distributed after your death. A will identifies who should receive what property. You can be as specific as naming someone to receive a particular piece of jewelry or a collection of books. You can also designate a guardian for your minor children, although the court reviews your request to determine whether it's in the child's best interest.

A trust can manage your estate before and after your death, which is why it's often defined as a "living" trust. Basically, you transfer your property to a trust, which then owns it. You can designate yourself as trustee and manage it while you're alive and able. You also choose a successor trustee to take over after your death. A trust is a revocable document; you can make changes as needed.

Laws vary from state to state, so be sure you understand those applying to you.

Do I need both a will and a trust?

You'll definitely need a will, because it addresses your entire estate. A trust may be beneficial, because it can provide certain tax advantages while you're still alive. A trust can distribute payments to heirs rather than in a lump sum, and it's more private since it isn't subject to probate court (although beneficiaries in your will are informed). If your estate includes largely real estate, a business, or art and antiques, you should consider placing this property in a trust where it can be managed according to your wishes.

A "pour-over" will may be necessary to account for property not covered in your trust.

What happens if I die without a will?

If you "die intestate," a probate court distributes your estate according to the laws of the state where you lived, regardless of what you may have desired. Also, any property not designated in your will goes through probate.

When should I consider updating my will?

You never know when your life will end, so it's important to keep your will up-to-date. When you start a family or acquire any property, you should automatically make arrangements for the people you leave behind. You can revise your will at any time and may want to do so after significant life changes, such as marriage or remarriage, divorce, births, or increases in assets.

What is a living will?

Though a living will is a legal document, it's not an actual will. Also known as a "health care declaration," it describes how you want your health care to be directed if you become unable to communicate your wishes. For example, you can complete a "Do Not Resuscitate" form. In some states you must be in a vegetative state before your living will takes effect. Other states require that you have a terminal disease with a life expectancy of no more than six months. Learn the restrictions in your state, and be sure to have the document witnessed. Finally, tell your family about the living will so they know your wishes and that the document exists.

Do I have enough assets to establish a trust?

If you have a net worth of at least $100,000, a trust is worth exploring. Talk to your estate planner, lawyer, or tax adviser.

Are there different types of trusts?

We've already described the revocable living trust, but there are several other forms of trusts:

Credit shelter trust. Also known as a "bypass" or "family" trust, this requires that you write a will leaving a portion of your estate to the trust. The remainder of your estate then goes to your spouse tax-free. You stipulate how the trust funds will be managed. You can take full advantage of estate tax law by stipulating that the money from the trust that's given to your spouse should be passed on to your children after your spouse's death. Since you and your spouse have separate estate tax exemptions, this effectively passes two estates to your children and bypasses the estate limit.

Generation-skipping trust. Also called a "dynasty" trust, this provides for grandchildren and great-grandchildren. You can specify how the funds will be used.

Qualified personal residence trust. You can give the gift of your home or vacation residence using a QPRT. This is a good choice if the property is likely to appreciate in value. You specify the length of the trust and can continue to use the residence. The IRS assigns a value to the residence, taking into account current interest rates, your life expectancy, and other factors. The calculation assumes the value will depreciate before your heirs take possession. The longer the term of the trust, the less the value of the gift. If you have a vacation home, for example, worth $500,000, it might be valued at $350,000 when placed in the trust. The home could have actual market value of $650,000 by that time, but the gift retains the lower value of $350,000 for tax purposes. However, if you're still living at the end of the term, the home assumes its full market value when it reverts to your estate.

Irrevocable life insurance trust. An ILIT takes your life insurance out of your taxable estate. The money can be used to offset estate costs or provide a tax-free income to your heirs. But after you transfer your life insurance to the trust, you cannot borrow against it.

Qualified terminable interest property trust. A QTIP trust is commonly used for a member of a family with divorces, remarriages, and stepchildren. The purpose is to ensure that your assets go to the family members you desire. You assign the assets to your surviving spouse and designate who will receive the remainder of the trust's assets after the spouse dies. For an effective tax shelter, create a bypass trust up to the estate tax maximum, and transfer the remaining assets to a QTIP.

How can I provide for charitable donations?

Charitable donations are a wonderful use of your assets. You can reduce your taxable estate by making a tax-deductible contribution to a fund that's like a cross between a mutual fund and a foundation. Your money accumulates tax-free interest through investments by the fund's manager. You can designate donations at any time to a charitable organization from within the fund, and you can take the tax benefit long before you actually award the contribution. Check all charitable funds for legitimacy.

A "charitable lead trust" receives the interest while the principal goes to your heirs. A "charitable remainder trust" reverses this; the charity receives the principal. Colleges and universities are often recipients of such trusts.

PLANNING FOR LONG-TERM CARE

People are living longer than previous generations, and the large baby boomer population is reaching its golden years. While many adults remain active and independent long after they retire, others face medical conditions that require increasing levels of care. Assisted living and residential care facilities provide comfortable housing and medical care, but they can be expensive. Long-term care could mean months, years, or the rest of our lives.

Do you have the ability to pay for such care? Will your family or loved ones be burdened with the task of financing your lack of planning?

Many people assume that their adult children can help with the caregiving. But is this a realistic expectation? Not if you realize that women are the most common caregivers, and about 60 percent of the 116 million employable women have jobs[13] and are therefore unable to provide full-time care.

How do I plan for long-term care?

Try to project your needs. Investigate the annual cost of a residential care facility. If you can afford it, incorporate this into your living will and discuss it with those who will be responsible for your care, particularly your health care proxy.

What is long-term care insurance, and how much does it cost?

This covers the cost of extended medical care without depleting your assets—and your family's inheritance. The premium will vary according to your age, sex, location, and policy type. The younger you are, the lower the premium. Expect to pay between $500 and $3000 per year. The cost may seem overwhelming, but when you compare it to the cost of home health care (approximately $12,000 per year) and a nursing home stay (averaging $70,000 annually[14]), this is a small price to pay to receive essential health care without emptying your bank account. The greater the coverage, the higher the premium, so consider carefully what services you'll need. If you're still working, see if you can get group insurance with your employer at a reduced rate.

How do I choose a policy?

First, make sure the policy is guaranteed for life (yours, that is) and cannot be canceled by the insurance company. Next find out what is covered and, more importantly, what's excluded. Is there a waiting period before you can receive benefits? What conditions will cause your benefits to take effect? How impaired do you have to be? Also find out the limits of your coverage. How long will benefits be paid? Is there a preexisting condition exemption? Is inflation figured into the benefits? The cost of living also affects the cost of health care, particularly with skyrocketing medical costs, so ensure that your policy will reflect these increases.

Also look at the company issuing the policy. Is it reputable? Has it been in business for a long time? Check the company's financial strength rating (FSR) with services like A.M. Best, Standard and Poor, Fitch, Moody's, or Weiss. The Insurance Information Institute recommends checking with at least two of these services. And consider getting a second opinion on the policy from someone on your financial team. The insurance salesperson may not be so objective.

Doesn't Medicaid or Medicare cover long-term care?

These two government programs are not synonymous with eldercare. Medicaid is provided to disabled and elderly people with low incomes. If you qualify, some long-term care might be covered. For example, some nursing homes will bill Medicaid, while others do not accept this insurance. And even where it's accepted, certain services may be excluded.

Medicare has no income restrictions, but coverage for long-term care is somewhat limited. Home health care may be available for a short time, but a nursing home is probably not covered. Long-term stays are considered custodial care and are unlikely to be covered by Medicare.

Visit medicare.gov to find out what's covered in your area; coverage varies from state to state.

ONE MORE WORD ABOUT YOUR RETIREMENT

Retirement planning is literally a matter of life and death. Aging is a fact of life and brings with it a new focus. Put fear behind you and face this now to make life easier later. You can live many years in retirement, so you should take the time to use your present resources to make those years as carefree as possible. After a lifetime of hard work, retirement is your reward. A retirement plan can be designed and managed without a lot of effort. Spend a little time now on your plan, and you'll have plenty of time later to thank yourself and, above all, God for the extraordinary vision for a leisurely, comfortable retirement.

You can smile at your future.

Acknowledgments

My first thank you, as always, belongs to God; the Source of all wisdom and the Provider of all answers to questions—dumb or otherwise.

I also want to thank my husband who is my financial partner and, more importantly, the love of my life.

To our children—thank you for encouraging and loving Mommy, even as I type away at my computer during the wee hours of the morning.

To my parents—thank you so much for being my role models and always being the first to read my manuscripts.

Much gratitude goes to my agent, Wes Yoder of Ambassador Agency, who truly loves the Lord and is committed to quality work in honor of Christ.

I adore the team at Multnomah Publishers including my incredibly talented editor, Thomas Womack; Don Jacobson; Doug Gabbert; Guy Coleman; Kimberly Brock; Chris Sundquist; Tim Nafziger; Natalie Johnson; and Bonnie Johnson. Special thanks to editor and researcher Jacki Payne, who has become my sounding board, and to my financial team: Attorney Kirk Levy; CPA Kim Painter, and Realtor Monique Summerlin.

A special thanks to the Christian Broadcasting Network and the wonderfully creative staff of *Living the Life*. I love working with all of you and especially taking time to pray and worship God during the middle of the day. As I've told many of you, most newscasters never get that privilege.

And to all of the people over the years who have endured my television and radio interviews and countless questions—many thanks for your answers in return and for helping to shape my thoughts and theories about taking charge of our money. May God bless all of you abundantly and eternally in Jesus.

Notes

1. National Association of Realtors 2004 Profile of Home Buyers & Sellers

2. *The Virginian Pilot*, March 15, 2006

3. Spiegel, Matthew, "2000 A Bubble? 2002 A Panic? Maybe Nothing?" som.yale.edu, October 28, 2002.

4. Edgerton, Jerry and Jim Frederick, "Build Your Wealth Drip by Drip," *Money Magazine*, August 1, 1997.

5. Figures as of 3/21/06.

6. For extensive additional references on copyright law including the actual US Codes go to http://fairuse.stanford.edu/ and http://straylight.law.cornell.edu/uscode/search

7. For a more extensive description of patent application requirements, see *Essentials of Intellectual Property* by Alexander Poltorak and Paul Lerner, published by John Wiley & Sons Inc., 2002.

8. Further information on trademark registration is available at the USPTO website: http://www.uspto.gov/

9. The USPTO provides a great deal of information on international protection of intellectual property rights on their website: http://www.uspto.gov/main/profiles/international.htm

10. Employee Benefit Research Institute 2005 Retirement Confidence Survey

11. According to figures from The Investment Company Institute, Washington, D.C.

12. Effective 2006

13. Day, Thomas, "The Need for Long Term Care Planning," longtermcarelink.net

14. 2004 MetLife Market Survey of Nursing Home and Home Care Costs

Index

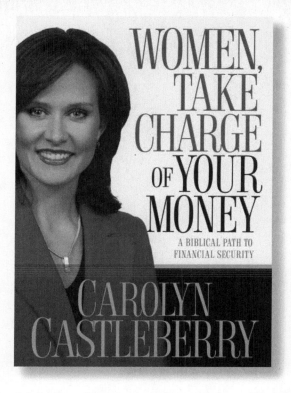

In her first book, *Women, Take Charge of Your Money,* Carolyn Castleberry provides a financial wake-up call and leads women through the process of creating, considering, and investing. With a conversational and easily readable style, Castleberry offers readers guidance on topics which include:

- Knowing their life's mission and where money fits in
- Understanding the basics of budgeting
- Creating an action plan for getting out of debt
- Savings-plan essentials and wise retirement planning
- The fundamentals of real estate, stock market investments, and estate planning

Women, Take Charge of Your Money is your ticket to a new life grounded in financial freedom!

Available at bookstores everywhere.

The Proverbs 31 E-newsletter subscription information:

The Proverbs 31 E-newsletter is a monthly publication sent to your email inbox. Your subscription is free with the purchase of this book; it will launch January 2007 and continue until December 2007.

To access your subscription, log on to Carolyn Castleberry's website: www.carolyncastleberry.com. Click on the icon for the newsletter. When you are prompted to enter a user ID, enter your email address. When you are prompted to enter a password, enter: TLS915.

For other great resources, log on to www.carolyncastleberry. com today!